waking red

an anthology

The Wild Matryoshka

ELIXIR PRESS
BOULDER, CO

Waking Red: An Anthology
ISBN: 9798300189150
Imprint: Independently published through KDP publishing
Book & Cover Design: Stasha Ginsburg
www.thewildremembering.com

waking red

an anthology

To fairytales and myths from around the world, and special thanks to:

Little Red Riding Hood (Grimm)
Briar Rose (Grimm)
Six Swans (Grimm)
The Lost Girl (Ojibway)
Vasilisa the Brave (Russian)
Selkie Woman (Celtic)
Women at the Well (Celtic)
Becoming Fox (Siberian)
Fox Woman and the Hunter (Siberian)
Cerridwen's Cauldron (Celtic)
Where Stories Come From, (Seneca)
The Question of Imagination (Hans Christian Anderson)

To the muses, the weavers of story;
To grandmother moon and her cycles.
To the 'well' ancestral wisdom woven through these words.
To the spirit of place, plants, elementals and puckwudginees.
To the 13th Fairy, the teachings of shadow, the hidden revealed.
To Eros, wild blooms, thorns and natural timing.

To the animal beings including but not limited to:
Wolf. Fox. Heron. Hummingbird. Spider. Hare. Hawk. Swan.

To the 13 women of the Crack Open the Story immersion May - July 2024. Your voices, courage, blooms, elixirs, words, truth, and personal mythos made me more whole.

Preface

waking red: an anthology.

Thirteen women. Thirteen weeks. Twelve Fairytales/Myths.
A thirteenth creation to emerge as this beautiful spinning wheel
of threads, poems and prose.

The fairytales and myths chose us.
The Question of Imagination (Hans Christian Andersen)
to awaken a new way of sensing, seeing and listening;
The Origin of Stories (Seneca),
to remind us about the necessity of feeding the story.
From there, we journeyed into Once Upon a Time
navigating fairytales, myths and folktales
of the German Black Forest, Siberian tundra, Slavic otherworlds,,
Celtic liminal mists and Ojibway puckwudginee groves
near the edge of an inland sea.

The process and the product, a verb and a title— Waking Red.
The red swallowed by wolf.
The red of wild red roses on the hidden briar patch.
The red of the noon rider on the path to Baba Yaga's hut.
The flaming red of creative fire and transformation from a skull..
The red drop of blood from the 13th Fairy's spindle prick.
The red of beauty's lips after a kiss.
The red sun opening the bud.
The red of persistence as a silent woman spins cloaks
to break a curse.

Red. Licking the red scent of eros in a fox tail.
Red. Becoming Fox. Tracking the red in Story.
Churning Cerridwen's cauldron and receiving the divine spark
of mythos on the back of the hand, burning churning
the wild remembering into the ruby red marrow.

How many shades of red is at the center of story?

Red Riding Hood led us into the dark belly of all that is
—lost and found, forgotten and broken, fractured and hidden,
secreted and revealed. Red. Great great granddaughter to
Persephone.

Devoured by the wild hunger of her own primal awakening.

Renewed as bold, brave Queen. Of her own story-myth.
Red, writing her way into wonder filled RedWolf writing.
Howling from inside her own belly as she claws her way out
with a new poem. Red retrieving herself and her stories.
Little Red Writing Hood tattooing new myths on birch bark,
bone and stone with the 13th fairy's spindle.

Each fairytale cracked open a mythopoetic orchestra of poetry
embroidering stars between the lines of well worn stories.
Rewriting the old story and repurposing it into a new constellation.

We live in strange times. Journeying into *once upon a* time is its own
path of awakening. Come as you are. Journey into the liminal.
Experience ordeals. Crack open a story. Retrieve something
forgotten, forbidden, fertile. Stories. Poems. Truth. Freedom.
Power. Discover self as you write across the bridge from the
personal to the mythic and back again changed.

The poems, voices, stories, testimonies, eulogies and revelations in
this collection are the elixirs from the mythopoetic call to adventure
Crack Open the Story, from May - July 2024. We met over zoom for
two hours to sing, witness, commune, hear fairytales and write our
way inside and out of them. These astounding women brought me to
awe and tears. These writings the harvest of the fruits of their labor.

Fairytale is a much needed water of life during times of change. Fairytales are moist with life -a chalice from the healing waters of the divine feminine. A nourishing balm for the dry, analytical, materialistic, mechanistic mindset that we have been cultured into. Fairytale and myth are potions and metaphorical medicinal RX. Women are naturally suited to eat, drink and sleep with them. I witnessed mythos glowing on the skin of these women as they wrote and spoke the words you are about to read.

The writers and poets in this collection were of many nationalities and wrote from and/or about diverse locations on the map -United States, Slovakia, Poland, England, Australia, Belgium, Germany, Morocco. It was a profound honor to witness and guide them through the path of story. Our writing journey was not only a transformative writing process, but also, a gift of sacred and renewed sisterhood. We became a living poem glistening with stardust, moss and morning dew.

May these raw, sensual, fierce and diverse voices stir the cauldron of inspiration in you. May you be sparked and enlivened. May the rose of beauty awaken and unfurl the red in you.

And so....we begin with the scent of something hidden, something forgotten, something lost, now found, emerging, remembered.

At the center of Crack open the Story.

There Blooms
Their Blooms

Natalie Britton

Natalie is an imaginative Leo-Gemini-Capricorn
in the process of healing generational trauma
and rising into her most connected, authentic self.

She is an educator and co-founder of Nova High,
a Waldorf-inspired high school based in Sandpoint, Idaho.

Natalie enjoys all creative arts, cultivating community,
running, spending time in nature,
and learning how to transform her 7-acre homestead
into a place of growth and nourishment.

You can find her spending time with her husband
and two young sons
somewhere in the woods.

BATTLE CRY

Dear Women,

I have a letter for you all. To me. To all sisters, near and far.

I never had a sister. Like, a blood sister. I've had a lot of chosen sisters, but they sort of flutter in and out of my life like transient butterflies.

What's it like to have a Real Sister?

For some reason, the fabric of my ancestral lineage can't hold sisters. There must have been a dropped stitch that gave way to a loose, lacy blanket that's really pretty to look at but can't hold shit. The women forgot their sacred bond and bled it all out between their legs and through the yarn, and the Great Body of whatever Great Mother birthed me could no longer hold onto feminine substance. The shamans call it "Feminine Implantation Failure."
It's why I had two boys and no girls.

But I am here, as a female.

We are here, my mythopoetic sisters.

Now that we're officially sisters, it's time for some honesty. Honesty is a medicine so deeply vital to the survival of the female species. So, here's a dose of it.

Throughout this transformational 10-week container, I have embarrassingly produced a negligible amount of writing.

To be honest, I have been fucking terrified.

I am a recovering perfectionist.

I was raised to know only conditional love from my mother. Were you? I was raised to attract the attention of my mother through performance.
Were you?

I was born to a mother who only knew how to connect by telling inflated stories of herself and completely withholding the hard, vulnerable stuff. Were you?

And if you weren't, no matter. I know you can still feel the poison in our collective well. I know you still can feel how all our deep and true beauty was cast as pearls before swine, how our wombs have soured in perversion.

And yet, here we are. Here we are, showing the fuck up and mastering the Art of Alchemy. This is why we're here, right? To restore the Goddess within. To transcend the abuse, to sanctify the twisted distortions that we've worn like ugly masks:

Big boobs. Small waists. Big lips. Small ears. Big butts. Small noses. Big eyes. Small chins. Big brows. Small bones.
Big and small in all the right places.
Big egos. Small hearts.
So easy to mold into whatever the hell Big Brother sees as a flawless appearance.
Flawless appearance.

Fuck that narrative.

Sisters, we are actually authentically truly FLAWLESS. We are fucking flawless.

We, in this space together, who endeavor to challenge the collective myth, who endeavor to face the She-Devil herself in the bathroom mirror, living in every "yes sir" and "give it to me baby" and "whatever you want, dear" ever uttered by muzzled lips.

We are Here doing the Work.
Shifting back to softness. Embracing desire. Welcoming the unknown. Falling out of our prison nests without a new nest to fall into,

Until we realize -

That the nest-less void we are falling into is

The FREEDOM

We have all been calling in

The FREEDOM

We are here to channel

And act upon

For all of the women

Who don't have conscious opportunities

To call anything in

Because they are all in survival mode,

As their grace is violated,
As their power is choked,
From them,
Sometimes even by them.

So let's LIVE,
And read dirty novels and compliment the hell out of each other,
Let's wear the most gaudy dresses,
Let's revel in everything girlishly gorgeous
without the weight of judgment or association,
Let's massage every bumpy lumpy part of ourselves
with infinite gratitude for what it is,
Let's drink the wine,
And eat the cake
Of life,
And jump out of planes
And call our mothers and tell them we forgive them
No matter how fucking mean they've been to us,
BECAUSE IT FUCKING IS - WE FUCKING ARE -
YOU ARE,
I AM.

Parting QUOTE:

From The Heroine's Journey by Maureen Murdock:

*"To awaken the divine feminine is to ignite the fierce, primal force
within us that connects us to the cosmic rhythms and the earth's raw,
untamed energy. It is to rise in our full glory, embracing our power
and wisdom without fear or compromise."*

Elaine Fitzpatrick

Elaine is a lover of books, nature, and cats.
She is an aspiring writer.

This is her first publication.

Untitled I

I have journeyed, am journeying
through landscapes familiar and unfamiliar
seen with new eyes
I sniff the air
ears swiveling
tail twitching
hitherto dormant senses awaken

awakened

I see the world as a kaleidoscope of possibility

I pad through the forest
my senses show the way
treading lightly on the ground

home and yet not home
the crisp air invigorates me
the smells intoxicating, stimulating

stars glittering
gleaming pinpoints to light
my world

Where do I go from here?
I am better equipped
re-wilding
re-awakening to my wild nature
to use my newfound hard-won senses
to navigate this old and new terrain
alike
anew

Forest Wisdom

In order to pursue who I am, must I give up everything that I know?
Settling for what I know, for what is familiar, is not living.
Go into the forest, you will find the answers there.
They may not be the answers you were looking for, but they are.
Their form may surprise you.

Peel back your cataracts, your eyes that have forgotten how to see. It
is still there, they know.

Brutal awakening. Alive and running from what we thought we knew
into the unknown.

Captured by fear! There is a way out. Listen to your voice. Keep
listening with all of your senses. They will tell you how to find your
way out.

Don the fox fur, smell what was hidden from you
before and move on it.

Dig dig dig dig dig
Deeper deeper deeper deeper deeper
until you make a passage you can fit through.

Run back to what you know, to what is familiar.

Except that it's not anymore.
You're changed and therefore everything has changed.

Take your final nourishment and go.

Return

Peace, sunlit glade
birds singing all around me
I let their song carry me away, into the warm light,
into the vibrant green,
into the soft quiet.

I travel through nook and crannies I would otherwise not have.
Surprising sharp bends, up and
down, duck and swoop, float and sink.

I let it carry me to wherever it leads.

Here I remain until the other world inexorably pulls.

Imbued with birdsong, golden sunlight, dancing roots,
the smell of green

I return.

Spinning

How long I have waited,
patiently spinning and spinning.

I can wait. I will wait for you until you arrive.

I will let you fulfill your destiny.
I will not hinder the future from coming.

And when you do, my purpose has been satisfied and I disappear.

My waiting is over and I am released.

Unintended

I work hard
every day
doing the lion's share
doing my duty for someone else
selbstverständlich

at the end of my arduous and -
let's face it -
boring task
I hurry a little
speed things up
quicken my tempo
almost there…

…and shit!
I got the gift
the unintended gift
the gift intended for someone else

I open
I see
I am

I AM ALL

shit!
she is pissed and is going to kill me.

run run run
change change change
more more more
why stop at a kernel?
life comes from a kernel
I can't hide forever
I will be digested and reborn

Healing

What needs healing is manifest
It is demanding and must be answered
What is it, my love? What caused your pain?
What can I do, what must I do, to heal you?

Show me the way.

Underneath

I am my ancestors and I am not my ancestors
I break the cycles
I release them and let them fly free
You are no longer needed

When they leave, underneath is a glow
A shining egg of gold and light nestled in the brown leaves
uncovered
palpable
pulsing

A nascent being who was always there
waiting patiently for you to find her

Purpose

Stories come to me, songs come to me
but meaning and purpose are elusive

I catch glimmers from time to time
a golden sparkle at the edge of my vision tingling my senses

A ha! There she is and there she goes.
Grab gossamer threads lightly
containing and contain the sparkle

Lightning flashes of insight

gentle
sudden
powerful
matter-of-fact

They were always there
waiting to be uncovered by a spark

Meaning and purpose ripening within me

unfolding
opening
sparking
lighting

Burning

Dull flame half-baked
glowing embers that refuse to die
glowing embers that are reluctant to meet oxygen
for it means burning life and all of its pain

Oxygen touches the embers and the flame ignites

Burning
burning for knowledge
burning for experience
burning to see
burning for love

The smell of smoke
sparks, crackles, comforting, calming, opening, invigorating

Fire is life
ever-changing flames lick and touch
they twine with the air
dancing
unfurling

Eyes and teeth glittering

The scent of smoke in my hair is perfume

Ache

There is an ache inside of me
I know not for what
a yearning for something I cannot name yet feel deep in my belly

I let the ache lead me to destinations unknown

Unfamiliar horizons

churning
flowing
trickling
falling

Where will my ache take me?

It has already taken me across the water.
pulling
yearning
cleansing
immersing
cooling
invigorating

The wind in the trees
the chatter of woodland
the sound of water

Journey

wandering wandering
taking in all I see
but not knowing the name of what I seek

until now

glimmer shimmers appear

reds
wolves
spindles
swans
selkies
flaming skulls
foxes

with courage
we shapeshift our way through

Liana Gerdov, Psy.D., CH.T.

Liana is a holistic, depth-oriented psychologist,
hypnotherapist, energy practitioner, Priestess,
and a bit of a time-traveler with past-life regressions.

She incorporates Internal family systems (parts work), inner child
healing, Jungian concepts, creative expressive arts,
and sprinkles in Earth-based spirituality, past life/ancestral healing,
shamanism, art/writing/creative expression,
as well as Goddess-oriented mythopoetry, folktales, divination,
& guided imagery in order to unveil the unconscious consciously,
weave together threads and pieces,
& integrate client's "worldly" experience
in a more soul aligned foundation
to bring forth long-term healing.

She is devoted to helping individuals
feel a sense of empowerment and connection
through rituals and ceremonies, magical crafting,
creative arts, empowered birth journeys, and retreats.

Untitled

The moment the king turned on his beloved
When he no longer believed her
When he no longer saw her
When the supportive barriers of his love and care
shattered to tiny little pieces all around her

What remained to be said?
Are there words to convey the deep and utter sadness?
Betrayed, angry, bewildered
Bursting with fierce fire of a dragon and at the same time
Constricted, small, heartbroken
How does one break generational curses, patterns
and other muck?

I just don't know

Silence

Silence
Seemingly golden
And yet, it can feel rotten,
leaving a nasty taste lurking on the tip of the tongue
I have been the keeper of silence for many
Gently rolling secrets into a neat little ball,
tucking it into the box and locking the key
Like any good ball of yarn, it starts to unwind,
to burst at the seams,
to lay out its own path
I have been comfortable in the silence
In the space
In the black hole
The thing is - whether it's a whisper or a shout
Sometimes our voices are still met with silence
Or our voices suffer an even worse fate
Criticized, misunderstood, ostracized
For so many lifetimes
The chains of silence feel so heavy
Hidden in the shadows. Silenced
Not by my own accord
But out of necessity and protection
What is the point of speaking your truth?
Of asking for help?
Of trying again and again?
Do I stay hidden in the shadows? In the ease and familiarity of it all?
Do I use all of my might to break free from the cold, dense chain,
one by one? I feel frozen, stifled, and drained
I want to lay down my shield and sword
Soar through the meadow
Whisper my truth to the hawthorn trees
and sing with the birds

In the Belly

In the belly, in the depth, in the darkness
Swallowed whole
I feel comfort, respite, peace
Pieces of me lay resting
Parts not yet integrated
But seen, and heard, and witnessed
In the witnessing
In the observing
Not yet knowing there is light on the other side
Not yet feasting in the transformation afoot
Not knowing how…or what…or when parts will emerge
In the silence
Sensing, sniffing, prowling
Held and nestled into an embodiment of Self
Thoughts drift off
In the timeless Liminal
Beyond the walls, there is a world full of possibility
A circuitry of building and shaping
Here in this moment, I listen to the ancestral rhythmic beat
Of my Heart
My Soul gently hums a tune
Remembering
Crocheting together infinite wisdom
While leaning into the mysteries of this gentle and warm cocoon
Here in this space of fluidity, of quiet and calm
I birth my voice
A call for reawakening

To gather
To listen
To pause

Before the cauldron is stirred again

A remembrance

Under the moonlit sky, we sit curled up
By the warm flames and rhythmic crackle of the fire
Smoky ash gently enveloping our bodies
Mesmerized, we gaze upon the dancing flames
Sparking an internal burning within
A dance
A wonder
The flames call upon me like a soft, sweet song
Wrapped around in the beauty, comfort, and enchantment of the fire
We sit
We chat
We listen
Truly, truly listen to our raw, open, collective souls
I sing a song that slipped,
ever so gently off of my tongue
I catch the words one by one
Slurp, slurp…pause
The dirt beneath my bare feet holds me, as it always does
I dig my toes slowly into the cold Earth
As if I was growing roots

"It reminds me of our connection with the Great Mother
and interconnection," I whisper to my grandmother.

"The cold Earth reminds me of the war. The famine. The spine
chilling fear
that consumed so many loved ones, friends and neighbors," she
whispers back, unable to hold back her tears.

The ash settles onto her open palms
as she reaches them out toward the flames
She shares stories of her brother

Her favorite brother
Who went off to war at seventeen and never returned
Words slipped off her tongue
Each one met with a pause
And a tear

She chokes up
As if the flames knew that it was just too much
Too much to hold
Too much to speak of

I take her hands and bring her palms together
Cocooning her hands into my small palms
I remind her that her brother is in every glimmering star around her
He shines upon her as the Sun comes up
Cleanses her spirit with the rain
Makes space and holds her with every step she takes
He is in every nook of the Earth
And in every cell in her body

We sit
Cradling each other
Humming
Swaying
Laughing
Crying by the fire

Held. Supported. Never alone.

Unfurling

I am the wild rose, opening up
Holding onto the wisdom of years
And years before
Curling up and going within
Finding momentary pause in order to unfurl
And open up
Sweeping away the old wounds, the fears, the misunderstanding

I wait
Knowing there is more to come
Beyond the stillness, the pause, the familiar resistance
Eager to explore what is at the edge
What dreams begin to unfold and fill my being with wonder?

Reflections ricochet from the mirrors of my soul
I push away and open each petal with all my strength
One by one, piece by piece

Soft, velvety knowing flows through my entire being
With each petal unfurling, the thorns melt and fall away

One step closer to new beginnings, adventures,
and newfound hope

Knowing that the power to awaken is within me

In my own time

At my own pace

Perfectly Imperfect

Perfectly imperfect
I see the world from a different lens
Heck, it's not even a lens at all
A labyrinth, a carnival, a mirror
A portal into the other realms
No beginning and no end
I get lost in time or rather, I time travel
Feeling into the deep and moist,
and sometimes slippery crevices of the core

I skip in a circle instead of walking the line
I whisper when others around me shout
My healers - great big oak trees, vibrant waterfalls,
and larger-than-life mountains

My inner and outer landscape knows no bounds
I stand proudly and firmly at the edges,
extending my arms and soaring

I bow down to the woman I once was

And fly

I lay you down to rest

The mountains are calling
Breathing life through me
Inch by inch
Reawakening me
The breeze rolls off my skin
I settle into the sacred temple of the Blue Ridge
It's heartbeat reminds me of my own

It calls to the little heart that merged within me
But only for a little while
Just sixteen weeks
Not enough time to spend together

I sing to you
Cradled by the giant rock behind my back
"What happened little one?" I whisper
as I swirl my finger into the earth's warm soil

I rest my bones here
By the mountain
I gaze at the songbirds
And the endless tree elders

I hum
I dance
As tears flow off my cheeks
and drop down onto the earth

I search for the piece of my heart
that forever merged with yours little one
As I lay your bones to rest

As I lay down all of life's little moments we could have shared

Gathering the threads

I am the dress that gathers
The little white dress,
holding bits and pieces of the strings
Knowing the sacredness of each little thread
Weaving each one into greatness
Weaving bits of stories
And memories
And mysteries

Each thread unlocking access to laughter,
joy, sadness, fear, anger
And everything in between

Threads - some jumbled up, ripped, tangled
Some perfectly lined up and interconnected
All nestle inside of the white cloth
Some days, they feel broken

I remind them of the ancient healing art of Kintsugi
Finding the beauty
in what is perceived as broken,
shattered and tucked away
Beauty and life hidden
in the mending, nurturing, witnessing

Laying out the path

Loving, healing, wrapping around with golden thread

Lien Lunefien Van Camp

Lien is moss loving storyteller
who delves up the pearl in chronic illness.
This wild elf living in the woods
inspires others to embrace their messy and marvelous
through expression circles, story, song
and rites of passage.

First time published.

Lost and found

I no longer have the illusion of living the fairytale perfect life. That by the age of 39 I would be a successful mom and storyteller, 2 children, a picket fence and a husband who would just be the perfect match because we had travelled the world together haha. I let go of that image I always drew when I was a child. Where there was a happy family with a giant tree near a little cottage with a swing, always a swing.

I could say I failed utterly. That I missed out on normal life completely by encountering severe chronic illness from the age of 17. Yes I lost many friends whose normal life no longer interested me. The only friends who stayed were the ones who travelled with me in the deep waters, nurtured by the soul food my illness lessons brought.

But then, at 39 I found a cute cottage in the woods with seven 250 year old inland oak trees and a little pond with mossy stones, glimmering with golden green sunshine magic. This color green is my always ultra super plus favorite color that in the human world only "*indigo ajuin aluin*" could match (indigo, onion skins with alum).It's the only colour that sparks the same joy as moss with the golden sun shining through.

I knew I could never decide anything without being dramatic and ponder ponder ponder as in a freeze and then just not decide.

Until now, for when I came here, I decided within 10 minutes "YES this is my home"as if it always had been.

Still figuring out where to put that swing though.

Stark naked, seeds and stirrings

What did I find in that cottage in the woods? I lost the romantic image of living off the grid. In dutch this is called *Zelf Voorzienend Leven*. (Self Provided Living). What I learned is that Self Provided Living is definitely not Provided Living by itself (*Vanzelfvoorzienend leven*. No, it is hard work.

I felt like living in the Wood sisters house, where - finally- my own hands could grow again, because even if I was ill, even if horrible headaches haunted me, the wood had to be chopped, holes had to be dug and chickens fed. Like in the Handless Maiden's tale, above my cottage is written:

"Here you can live freely." And that I did.

I was no longer constrained by images of how I should be. Of what I should be able to do or achieve every day. Here I could roam freely stark naked (*poedelnaakt)* in my garden, taking all the time in the world to listen to where the plants wanted to root. Being a full time guardian of nature.

I used to scream to my body : Heal! Heal! Heal! And when it wouldn't, when I had to cancel yet another fabulous adventure. I thought my soul really wanted to go on but my body couldn't, anger changed little by little in a deep bitterness. Maybe more on that later, or maybe I can choose to focus on the seeds and stirrings of new life energy.

In the 3 years in the woods I quietly let go of some of that impatience I felt towards my body. I saw that, no matter how much water, love or care I gave to a little plant, he could just grow as much as he could in a year.

41

That bush of last year grows stronger, bigger and belongs more to this earth, to herself this year. Only after a full year she rooted down as the plant she always was meant to become.

And so am I, little by little.

Inner and outer man

After a tough break up and my father dying, I felt so utterly lost. Like a chair on 2 legs. That habit of not trusting a man anymore, was a tough one. But I looked at it, felt it and realized, who knows, maybe I might trust a man, only if his ideas proved to be better than mine ? How could I know if I didn't let him try?

I noticed something strange: Living in the woods on my own appeared to appeal strongly to the imagination of almost any man near his midlife crisis. I had to sort out diligently like Vasilisa, and figure out: who was approaching me out of an interest in the real me who was just projecting all the things he never dared to live freely? One man was sure he saw a wild, independent wood elf who would definitely transform into an elm tree by night. Another was a bit afraid of that luscious wicked wood witch, though he would never admit it. Some dared to look closer and found a helpless girl who had no idea of how to build a shed that wouldn't crumble and was in desperate need of a father figure. This activated the rescue gene in some men. I didn't mind, though I really tried not to show that vulnerable girl but the challenges of the cottage made that almost impossible.

Especially that defining moment. It was the evening after we had finally repaired the roof from leaking. I was so relieved and proud and I felt a high Skip in Joy coming up while stirring in my soup.

So I hopped. And then...the kitchen floor under me just ..vanished. I got stuck in a hole of green, purple, yellow and even blue mold...and under that..the icy cold frozen January forest soil. Did Miss Panic take over? Yes, for a couple of minutes I wept and screamed and cursed all that was and all that was greater than me. But then I started laughing, cackling unstopping for an hour. I still had no idea how to solve that huge hole in my kitchen in the middle of January but somehow laughing was the only medicine in that moment.

Day after day I started to lose some of the habit of feeling lost, of missing out, of feeling utterly helpless. There were fewer days of "Miss Panic at anything unexpected." Something faded from the habit of always believing the worst scenario would definitely happen to me and no one else.I found new words, like *pop rivet*. Every man that came to help brought a new mantra, as an antidote for Miss Panic. Not to forget the teachings of Old Papa Youtube. Everything has a solution and if the solution hasn't arrived, it's just not finished yet. There's always another way.What really is a priority now? You can't do it all at once Lien. Finding creative solutions for unusual problems can be fun.You might not succeed at the first round and that doesn't make you a failure. Follow the direction in the wood, don't go against it.

Found new qualities in men. How creative they are, how persevering. How much that body can carry. Lost interest in highly educated men, for in university, you and I didn't learn how to live. Was turned off by fancy musician artists with great dreams but two left procrastinating hands.

I found other green flags. A man who knows how to use his hands in many ways. The way he has his way with wood. How he caresses it, how he goes into the direction of the wood as if he were caressing his only woman.

As if he's looking forward to playing a tune no one has played before on this cello hidden in that piece of wood, hidden in this woman's body.

I learned that telling a man exactly what to do and how to do it, doesn't necessarily mean you can immediately discern you have a great man before you. Can I let him do it his way? I could listen to a man who gently told me, Lien, anything is possible, it really is but, wood elf, on this earth you need to take into account gravity and how to build in a way that sustains you in the long run, not just because it's more beautiful and "elfy-hobbity" this way. Could I consider that maybe, just maybe my idea was born out of the stress of survival? Could I come down from that fairy place where time doesn't exist or where form changes rapidly?

I started to remember that on this earth, in this realm, form and healing is slow....And so here we are, after three years of being lost and being found.

O thank you for your teachings, you Great Masculine in me and before me. I welcome you, my inner man who can take care of me. As if the teachings my father never could or would or had the time and energy to give me, grew inside me. As if he sent all these different helping men my way to teach me all the things he couldn't. Little by little I built a new relationship with crisis. That feeling of invincibility. If I can handle these 3 years (this flood, this mold floor, this fire), I can handle anything. Nothing can shake my trust in a solution. I felt I wanted to anchor this transformation, so I bought a Hat. A hat that makes me feel I can handle anything,

because I earned those stripes

Selkie skin

I am the skin that brings you home.
I am the skin that nurtures all your cells,
that makes your body remember
the smooth wet fluid dance of who you are .
I am the skin that feeds all the empty cracks in you,
an oasis in your desert deserted body.
There is a way to feed your deepest ache.
Open your pores to my medicine.
Just come home.

You are my daughter. You can be in both worlds.
You can bring sea wisdom to the shore.

Embrace

I could finally feel
The Great Mother
Around me again

The mighty mountain

I lost my dad to his unrealistic dreams.
I lost my dad but I found a very imperfect one.
One that was a hero in being an anti hero.
Trying, falling, failing.
Getting up and starting anew.
That is what I learned from you.

But also the deep sigh. The deep sigh of depression
The gap between the Great Dream and Reality.
That sigh tries to bridge that gap, but never succeeds.
Because maybe the reality that comes, is the fulfilling of a dream you
once had, but forgot.
Or it is the dream you need, to grow.
Maybe it is the kind of trouble the 13th fairy had in store for you.
The Right Kind of Trouble.

For you can learn a lot from a father who was good at
transforming failure into an art form
Maybe I can realize my health dream in small steps
where only I see the victory
of a thousand tiny steps
climbing a Mighty Mountain in my Microcosmos.

Sleep, wake me

What is it in me that suddenly falls asleep?
When I fall asleep a part of me wants to melt and merge
in Morpheus's arms.
Asking Vasilisa's doll for guidance,
for tomorrow is always wiser then today.
I want to surrender, letting go of tension, resetting.
The fear of the deep makes me fall asleep.
Is it my life force that really needs resetting?
Or are there other ways to stay awake?

Who lies hidden deep within me?
This sorceress.
This fearless redheaded wicked wood witch
who is free.
How can I hear what you have to say?
Teach me other ways to hear you than sleep.
Let me ask the right questions.

Who will come to wake me?
Waiting for a man. Yes you woke me, by embracing all of me.
The pain and the armor. The messy and the marvelous.
You wake me by loving all that is.
So I can melt into who I really am beneath it all.
But only when the wild roses are ready to bloom.
And I somehow hate it that it is you,
because I have to wake myself,
don't I? Or do I?
Can I count on my inner man to wake me?
And do you really wake my deepest self
or can only I do that?

That deepest place

Calm open brightness, the stillness embraces all.
I hear the thorn hedges growing, protecting me,
protecting my sacred sleep.
I have slept so many days of my life.
I let the thorn hedges grow now. I don't let anyone in anymore.
Only those who understand the still center, can rest in it.
That deepest place.

The garden of silence is Eden.
Where the wild roses grow and bloom.
The scent envelops her as a mother,
as the mother she always needed.
Transforming her pain into peace

Life force

O Breath in my lungs, activate my life force.
Bring back my galloping fiery horse
Feed my organs. Open me.
You are the ebb and flow of my inner sea.
The rhythm that carries me.

Let her in breath not be too long,
always take time for the out breath in song.
Breath in all magic and give it roots
so she can offer her exuberant fruits.

Briar Rose. Nature decides.

She fell deep within herself. Everything stopped.
What did she dream?
What gestated, what ripened in her?
Many tried to wake her,
many tried to get through her thorns
but in vain.

A hundred years passed.
Only then – the wild roses bloomed- not a day earlier.
Only when she was ready she awoke by the prince's lips.
By the lips of time and tide, for nature decided it was time.
Nature always decides.

I needed 4 years. No contact with the outer world possible.
What gestated, what ripened?
I don't yet quite know but sometimes
all that heals is nature and time.
And silence. Deep silence.
Silence filled all the rooms in the centre
and all the spaces within herself.
A silence so vast it was heavy with possibility.

After she woke she was never afraid of being alone again,
for silence was a cloak that carried her, always.

Eulogy

Here lies the one who thought illness was all she had.
She lost her belief in cures, in a way out of this messy undigested
mush for the illness still served a purpose for her.

She thought it was the only way for her to belong.
If only she was sicker than her mother
she would finally get her attention,
her loving embrace and her special care.

She felt broken by life
and lost the belief in bending or mending.
How could she belong to nature,
for no one understood what was going on.
Nature would send the snails to finish what was weak.
So why was she still here?

She knew despair and bitterness so well.
Lost her trust in life, in ritual.
Her grief, her pain was the biggest
and could not be held by others,
so she thought.

And all that time she wasn't aware
of the pearl in the making
deep inside her grief body.
If only she knew how to fish it up
polish it and show this pearl of value to the world.

She had forgotten she belonged, just by being her.

It is done now. Rest in peace.

The elixir

I am the cauldron that digests it all.
All the tears, the rage and bitterness,
the longing, the lost feathers and the mud.
The phoenix and the broken bones.
The lost hope and the darkest desires.
I can digest it all if you are willing
to stir me for a year and a day.
Nothing is too intense or overwhelming for me.
Try me. I am the container that contains it all.

Give me your blood sweat and tears.
They all matter. They are all indispensable parts
of the potion that will become the inspiration of Awen.
Her darkest days, her throat orgasm,
the words that never dared to be spoken,
the heavy lead she wanted to transform into gold.
The nights she gave up and the days she felt invincible.
Her purple shoes, her swan wing, the red cape,
the black swamp and the blue sea.

At first a stinking bubbling mush.
By stirring long enough
it transformed.

She added a whiff of love,
a liter of acceptance,
a vase of vulnerability.
The stirring gave oxygen to the essence of the story
so it could breath and with the right incantation and song
her *elixir* was born.

The well women

How I would want to give the Sacred Water to the King.
A King that is worthy. Is there one ?
I want to guide the King together with my well maiden sisters
back to Sovereignty.
I want to tend a well, a sacred well.

It is time to come out of hiding, Sisters
to unite as Well women
to show our sacred white dresses
Claim our innocence again
Be healed.

In the belly of the wolf

Everyone is having a life and I'm in the belly of the wolf again,
missing it all. But what is here? Blackness. Wet softness. It is safe in
a weird way not being able to get out. I don't have to put myself out
there in the world to prove I am worthy of being alive. You are
enough just as you are now, here, laying in your sacred rest bed in
the belly of the wolf. Can I just stay here? But what if I come out and
I didn't learn anything from it, I just slept my life away? Can't breath.
No room. No space. Can't leave. Where is the light? What is here?
Grandmother. Hey Grandmother, can I just lay here with you and
forget the world?

Can you hold me?

The blackness of not knowing is also full of possibilities, she says.
Are you missing it all? Or what are you missing here and now?
This is where you are so this is where you learn.

Reborn out of the belly

I came out. I just came out of that dark deep belly
full of drama and pain story, smelly
Still feeling a bit discombobulated.
But I know there is a place for me, the daughter
amongst the wild souls who are not afraid of deep waters.
I am Red and what can I set free?

I carry you, dear body
I carry your scars like talismans, tattoos that strengthen me.
Every scar of every operation holds a secret key
to speak my wild truth in every breath.
Do you have a scar from your journey in the belly, Red?
Do you wear it with pride?
For we know, you never come out of the liminal fire belly
without being able to show it.

My relationship with food is ready to be reborn.
Nurturing doesn't have to be eating a pile of corn.
Small things can be food. Like Vasilisa's thimble of soup.
My body remembers how to heal me, breath me
So I can trust her and she can trust me.
For I am Red and I know my hunter can set anything free.

My inner queen, the queen of all things is back
and you listen to her, organs, for she is whole
and she knows what is needed to unpack.
Spleen, the danger is gone, you can digest the indigestible neatly.
It is safe to take in life completely
Work together to honor and feed her,
We need her. There is a fire in my belly that I am willing to feed.
A fire that digests all that lives here, with ease
So delightful to have all the organs working together for me.
For I am Red and I know I can set myself free

13th fairy

13th fairy what do you have to say about pain? You've had a lot of pain in your life. It seems unfair, doesn't it? Why you and why so much and why so long? *Because I knew you could handle it, daughter.* But I want to live, to do what I'm here to do!

That's what you're here for. To spin your straw into gold.

13th fairy, how to handle the pain, the limitation? So many things I want to do but can't right now. Panic feeling of panic everything goes so fast and I go so slow. O will you help me unravel my thread?

You can do it your way.
It's ok to have a life that others don't understand.
You can breathe, always breathe.

13th fairy, what do you know about despair? Of having everything taken away? Friendships, relations, health, wealth. How do you find the courage? What do you feel supported by when the world has forgotten the magic of 13, the magic of stillness and darkness? 13th, how do you deal with loss?

Let the moss carry you.

13th fairy, do you also feel bitter sometimes? How do you make bitter sweet again? *You can't. But you can transform it into something at least digestible, compostable .* Do you feel allergic to naivety too, like baba yaga? O I can feel such a disdain for innocence. Angels and little *waadidaadi* cards that will solve everything. Do you feel this loathing too for your happy happy fairy sisters? That are so horribly happy with their perfect life so they can only wish for perfect things because only love had found them?

If only you knew, pumpkin. O all the beauty. It has no ground if
your roots haven't grown in the deep dark mud of despair.
Only because of your pain can you enjoy life deeper, anywhere.

13th, I feel like I lost my innocence. How to ripen the lost innocence
with experience so it becomes wisdom?

Remember those purple shoes you so desperately wanted as a child?
Remember that feeling of invincibility and magic when you came on
the courtyard and then everybody laughed at you and called you a
witch? You resisted the colour violet for a long time later in life. It
was a colour you couldn't show, because then it was written on
your face that you didn't belong to this world, to these people, that
you were a witch. But, Lienie, said the 13th, I was the one who
inspired you to buy them. To reclaim your innocence, find the girl
with the violet shoes. She knows the way.

What do you want purple little wise girl? You could buy me
something purple or put it on your altar, to honor me, that little girl
who knows exactly who she is and what she wants:

> *I want to feel the magic of life.*
> *Be fed by it.*
> *And feed it in others.*

The wicked stepmother

I was there from the beginning. Her mother and grandmother had my elder sisters in their bellies. They all had them in their grasp so it was an easy vacancy. In all the places she didn't embody herself I could RAVE. Especially in her belly, for it was filled with cobwebs and dark slime anyways. No one was living there so I made my nest and stayed. I ate everything she had forgotten, anything she didn't want or couldn't digest. Her despair and powerlessness as desert.I spit my bitter gal everywhere. I took over her gallbladder for her judgment was off. I want her o put Netflix on and eat eat eat until she bursts. See? Told you you can't do it. It will never change, just give up. That's my curse.

But why?

I wanted to protect her. From what? If she had to feel all the grief all at once of all the shattered dreams, she wouldn't have been able to handle it. Bitter is safer. I protected her from her worst harm. From what? From being so goddamn naive. Against being broken by sadness. Better to build walls, they are stable, safer. Big walls with barbed wire, test them, test them 3 times. See if they can survive my poison. Poison for me means poison for her. That's only fair. I only wanted to protect her.

Did you now? I am not so sure but thanks for trying. For a long time I believed you. But I don't trust you anymore. Get out of my belly, get out of my gall.

Oh she could be naive so goddamn naive. she would really believe anything, especially if it was packed in a sweet voice that said he would protect her. And every time she didn't see what I knew from the beginning : this will end in tears, she cannot trust him.O how I cursed her innocence, her naivety. Grow some hair on those teeth. Be less dependent. Better to be independent and bitter than dependent and so vulnerable you melt and don't exist anymore. In the end she believed me. That no man can be trusted. It was easy for she had learned from the best. My elder sister who taught her mother could make especially bitter potions, nothing sweet to it. I knew for I had to make a poison that tasted at least a bit sweet so she wouldn't think she was exactly like her mother. No, this poisoning had to go slow.

O she tried to resist me. She became so goddamn sweet as a weapon. My elder sister's spitfire had made her mother independent and bitter, so she succeeded at driving all neighbors, all possible help and all friends away meticulously. And then little Lien would do exactly the opposite. She would trust everyone immediately and be such a sweet 'honneponneke', even when they trampled her boundaries, did she even have any? She didn't even know she was allowed to have them boundaries. Cover everything with the cloak of love. Because that is what innocent girls do, right? Whatever you do, don't become bitter like mama. Ha and there I saw a chance to strike. That potion finally worked! The more she tried not to become like mama, the more bitter she became.

I want her to stop writing. Because writing exposes me. I want her to do all the useless things first. Lately she is doing these breathing exercises. she is taking up more space and there is less space for me; So I put up a fight. I spit gall wherever there is room left wherever she isn't embodying herself. She found story. she danced all that she was, she even invited the 13th fairy and Baba Yaga with her piercing skull. O I don't like that skull. It just keeps watching me. It burns me. I can't do anything sneaky anymore or she has seen it.

She's burning me, and I become ash...sh...sh...sh

Be gone, evil stepmother, I burn you to ashes, let the fire transform you into something better, something new.

Pledge

I long to inhabit
my deepest depth again.
Like a treasurer,
delving up what wants to be seen and shared.
Stories, I' m back.
I pledge to honor you, nurture you
all of you who live inside of me.
They are not too dark.
Nothing is too dark for Mother Earth.
She can turn anything into compost.
It just takes
Time.
Waste.
Water
and trust.

The path

You can pick up a torch and light your way,
even though the path hasn't been walked before.
Or maybe it has, in an old story,
maybe it will, by someone not yet emerging
and maybe someone's path will be easier
because of how you walked till now.
I pledge to listen to you, mistress Moss.
To let my tears feed you,
to let me be fed by you.

The new story

You don't want the new story to emerge, do you?
A part of you wants to stay where you are, don't you?
You want to yell "I am not ready !"
NO. I have listened to you long enough.
There is a new story ready to emerge.
I am retrieving myself piece by peace.
The throne room of my soul isn't muddy or lost
I just have to dust a bit here.

> *My heart knows the way home.*
> *There is a way out,*
> *for there was a way in.*

Curious about the life above water.
Untangling forces, miracles, I welcome you.
There are ways, different ways

> *to digest*
> *to belong*
> *to 'medicinize' this life*

You have learnt so much
This cauldron that you are can contain you.

> *You are a blood sweat and tears sister.*
> *All your inner deep life fluids are welcome here.*
> *Story medicine will carry you.*

A year from now, this day will feel like a big leap. Remember:

> *How you deciphered the code of your mysterious body.*
> *How all the dead energy stuck in you was freed.*
> *How you created paradise in your outer and inner garden.*

Remember how you found the way.

Wendy Lindahl

Wendy (Samia) Lindahl, Sufi named of "Samia" for her gift of deep listening, follows the winds of Body, Dreams and Songs, uncovering wisdom within and beyond. A Dance Therapist, Body Whisperer and Intuitive Reader, she shares her original Dream Guidance process and leads dances and music for the Dances of Universal Peace.

Passionately rooted in offering classes, rituals, ceremony and wellness, while creating a doorway for others to follow their sacred paths at Mii Amo Spa for 18 years at Sedona's Enchantment Resort. Wendy also finds joy leading community singing. By the creek, you'll find her swimming, and playing her flute and guitar. At home she loves crafting mandalas, writing, gardening, hanging with her cat Azima and savoring healthy creations.

Guided by Stasha and inspired by the courage of women's stories, Wendy feels her spirit transformed and her heart braver, forever grateful for this shared journey of "Waking Red."

Spider Woman

I have been given these hands who love to create, to design,
a thread that has been in me since the beginning.
Made to reach out from my inner design
in holy spirals and rays of light.
Spider woman sings in me
as she spins silk into songs
that flow out onto the wind to catch
all the melodies I might hear and share.
It is the thread I carry in these hands
that I can trust to hold space, stretch time,
create containers of healing
for tears to spill and hope to return

for those parts of me and others
that thought we were alone to feel
woven through our dreams
into the web of kindness and contact
with all that is in this mystery
of belonging.

Singing over Her Bones

I remember telling my friend in a last breath conversation between us
that I would keep singing for her weary bones, a skeleton of who she
was before he stripped her flesh and ate her spirit. Her last words to
me before he shot her were "keep singing" …

now I sing for us both.

Why I Write

I write to hear what's within to honor and connect
to hear the truth that sometimes spills out.
A journey within into the forest of now
through all the depths and unknown paths.
I write to find myself,
to find my way
following only the mystery.
Not to expose but to nest and rest inside
and remember, I am welcome here.
Held in mycelial belonging
connected to what I am hungry for.
Silence, and awe.

To listen and become part of the ancient resonance
to offer this to my day and life
to the possible future that holds peace, reverence and belonging
as a vibration that sings
through my forest
and into the heart of humanity.

Body Cartography

Swallow swallow
really me? Ehem mmm …

I'm listening …

I'm not ready. I'm scared.
It's not always been safe. You know I can get you in big trouble…
Your just too loud, too brash, too intense.

No wonder this big lump, like a ball of yarn,
knotted and tightly wound
bright orange and red exists within my throat.

*Hey could it ever be a knitted muffler that could warm and welcome
rather than stifle or steal my true voice?*

True love awakens my nearly forgotten aliveness.

I am newly awakened willingly and innocently
curious to the sound of the spinning
hearing those footsteps again.
Tirelessly committed I spin and design
the most glorious patterns ready to awaken.

It reminds me, I am spun of this woven yarn
and remake the golden threads of what I have not yet known.
No longer asleep

I rise with what was forbidden and dangerous
now threaded to truth and doing what I am here to do
spinning like a dervish and ecstatic to play my part
in this glorious life I am here to create.
Lila Hu

Home

Ran away.
Swept by the wind and green.
Left home to find home.
To return to ancient roots of sacred groves
where my essence can be met.
Met and held, adorned hair in oak leaves and wild flowers
feeling the moss barefoot at creeks edge.
I know the flow, that of which I belong.
No turning back or longing for what was in city life
and the demands of family expectations and hopes.
Did I run away or let the wind carry me
to the trees that hold me and know me?
The blue heron standing regal where she belongs
and I too, I'm here in magical Sedona at Creek's edge.
Hear the mother Sycamore song
held and home.

Nest

Somewhere deep in my belly down in my bones
with heart wide-open, I enter the thicket of all that is stirring.
A bright colored small yellow bird perched, breaking off leaves,
and intent on creating a place a space, a home,
a nest for what is being born.
Singing, sweet tunes all the while in preparation for what is coming.
Adorning home in multicolored ribbons of natural wonder
I lay the foundation top down. The weight will be key,
the eggs number unknown still,
but held and layered possibility for the new.
Ready, not a cage,
but a nest for next.

Savage Daughter

I'm telling you for the last time child …
clean it up,
get organized and take care of your stuff.
You need to stay here.
Why do you have to run around so much,
you don't need to travel abroad.
There's so much to do around here
and why would you backpack or camp
you'll just get ants in your stuff and in your backpack
and then you'll bring it home dirty.
Be Careful! Don't get hurt, I worry for you and this is love.

When I was a child, I didn't have all that you have.
I took care of my things. I was responsible,
 the eldest child of three and needed to take care of them too.

I was my mother's helper as she needed my mothering too.
She was like a child herself, so I didn't get to be one.
Now you, you were to be my mother's helper,
but you are too free to tame,
too creative too independent and social to settle for this script.
I'd hoped if I loved you for being my mother's helper,
you'd lose your selfish ways, want less, accept the role and my love
as enough.That's all I ever wanted you know…

My own mother's love, but she was starving herself.
She migrated early on.

Hungry for mothering, and like the baby birds waiting to be fed
I could not afford to wait but became a clipped winged fledgling
and the nest she built I needed to help strengthen. She flew from far
away lands and didn't know the songs or the best tree or building
materials, twigs and leaves for our nest, I helped her and I only
wanted my girl to be like me.

But you had full brightly colored wings and a very deafening cry to my ears. So I couldn't and wouldn't listen I wanted you domesticated and caged like I was early on and my best attempts were not enough. You wanted to fly to travel to escape, and it scared me. You scared me because I saw what I could never become in your freedom and flight,

oh dear mother, may my flight give you both the mothering nest and the freedom you never had.

Fire Quest - Life on Mars

I am on a quest for fire to find the warmth and heat again.
Passion purifying and thumping heart, pounding my brain and bones.
One day I knew that the fires I was facing
in the land of the blazing sun was too hot!
I wanted cool blue water and green worlds
to nurture my scorched and parched being.
Beware of living on Mars
where you can't find your own fire any longer.
I was burnt and burned and unable to breathe
through the putrid smoke, orange suns
and dreams that came and went
as if suffocated in the mask of trying to make it OK.

Dreams like that want to be rekindled in a brand new beginning
anywhere but on Mars
I wanted cool green worlds
to nurture my scorch and parched being.
I searched and swam into vast oceans
where I could breathe again.

In this vision I set sail.

A New Spell is Cast

A "Huggy Brother" she called him
the potent arms of another
to feel that heart to heart appreciation
one soul with all its joy and heartache
held by another reflecting only a sense of "I got you"
and "you are not alone"
a hug became a kiss, the call of Eros
whispering feather kisses on my neck and ears,
kissing my forehead and eyes closed closer breathing,
kissing the tears of sleeping beauty awake.

Now I hear his voice like music from another time
and a far away place
when there were eons of time
and vast oceans of sound
that swept through like warm soft breezes
and we sailed the waves
to the pleasures of surrender,
trusted and let go of the shore following the currents,
the music the highs and lows.

Eyes closed kisses,
feather whispers there there only now now now
each moment a gift.
We float in a new sea
awake again, a new spell is cast.

The curse broken to be loved, seen, held, lifted
remembering all that was lost and forgotten
fated away left behind in a fairy dream that ended eons ago and
I can't remember how or why
but that was when I fell asleep,
the music and the Muse

Cursed to forget what Harmony feels like
on the skin and in my bones.
I am starting to wake up and dream again.
Feeling the starlight of my original form,
returning returning slowly slowly from this ancient slumber.
Soon, I will be a shimmering star again.

Wasteland

So much flow
just over there
I am here,
I've lost my Selkie Skin and memory of courage
caught in a tide pool eddy of same but different.
Now merely human
caught in this comfort again.
Beware of how this swirling comfort becomes sludge.
slowly sinking spirit, drowning longing.
Grateful for comfort
longing for flow.
What is new and fresh
ready to swim and
return to the slipstream
I'm finding my Selkie Skin
returned by the Savage Daughter and Fool
to make the plunge now
stinging cold pain just this moment
waking me up to my true aliveness again.

Grief

I grieve the long-held story of happily ever after
all the romantic notions of knights in shining armor
and soulmates beloveds that were in each other all along.
I've given up on true love and my innocent hope
that there is another who is "the right one".
I've been awakening from that dream
and I grieve it again and again
until I am no longer longing.

The perils of longing

Longing is something I am now seeing as dangerous the never
enough or unmet desires.

The once was great feeling of "having" the satisfaction the hunger I
didn't even know I had, met only to find myself desperate for that
magic again and again denied from what I long for, needing to wait
for once again I am a screaming child regressed to a version of me I
loathe, more more more.

Hysterical obsessed tantrum under my skin to have to wait and then
the relief when my thoughts aren't hijacked by this demanding
child's cries. Time soothes insanity don't listen and she will stop
crying. That's what the doctor told my parents don't come in. Don't
soothe her, let her scream long and hard until she is all cried out.
Fucking doctor Spock advice that left me confused on whether it's
OK too long for anything at all.

Water

My mouth thirsty for the purity of the natural spring waters,
ready to be nourished blessed recovered,
cleansing the toxic, political, and fearful places
that I have been drowning
in the last days, weeks, months.

Wanting to know, hoping for truth,
I tune in to the debates and commentary,
satire and ire humor of it all.
All men …where are the women who tend the deeper wells and
springs? Those of honor and care protection of soul.

I long to drink from these wells.
Have we all been devoiced and devalued?
Now I hear their poetry calling me home. Unmasked,
Selkies back in their skin, Red Foxes
and luminous weavers of stars.

To drink words from this spring
is to reconnect to what truly fills,
soothes and cleanses me
from what I have ingested
that I can't allow to dismantle my being.

Gentle hands placed on my heart
she whispers in my ear

come home sister friend.

Dare!

Do I dare pray for peace aloud.
Do I dare share what soothes and comforts
my worried, fearful and cynical mind.

Do I dare remember
my hopeful longing for a loving and just world?

Do I dare break the silence
when some may see me as a pipe dreamer
out of touch with reality, naïve.

Do I dare not take a step toward hatred and claim my own voice
for a vision that is honoring of the soft front, strong back
intelligence.

Do I dare not wither
in the face of true evil but stand strong in my resilience
to continue to love and live what I stand for.
To have compassion for myself
and all this soul smothering, snuffing out suffering.

Do I dare reserve my energy
wasted on battling against what feels unjust
and drink from a pure source of devotion to goodness and beauty?
To dwell in the poetry, mythology and music
that allows my wise, private wishes
and our collective dreams to take flight.

Do I dare remember
and listen to the dolphins playing and birds song.
Open to see the bright colored fuchsia yet delicate, blossoming
hollyhocks willing to grow and open even in the heat of summer, in a
pot, unlikely but here ready to dare to be itself.
I dare to be myself.

Water Song

♪♪♪ oleaha oleaha oleaha Hu.

Oh sweet, cleansing water
hold me
rock me
in waves and ripples.
Come inside me and baptize me with the memories
of love divine.
The ones that remind me that it is real.
The love that can heal all heartbreak and is more than human.
Springs of my blue grotto past carried
floated and restored to holy wholeness in your song.

Eulogy to Fear

Farewell to you, old friend,
Goodbye to the way you've kept me safe from judgment,
told me I am too much, too big, a show off.

Au revoir to your big pressing hands on my rising stature
that have been placed inside my bones and make me shrink
just so no one is uncomfortable.
Just so no one is threatened
or compares themselves to my greatness and aliveness.

I can't remain held in for fear of how I am perceived,
but claim my meteoric strength and creative essence,
bursting and ready to explode

Rest in peace,
voice of too much
in honor of more!

Stripper Siren

Meteoric lights flashing in rhythm to the beat of my heart.
Held in infinity
Slower, Faster, Wider, Deeper
Sun and moon alchemy
I follow flow, bones and cells merged.
Seduced into the fluid unfolding of becoming.
Breath by breath I AM
Inside out.
I am not an I anymore
but a thumbing
strumming
beating
ecstatic implosion
Holy Creatrix,
Faceless nameless
hair wild, body ablaze
shoulders shimmy, breasts alive, hips heave
Being swallowed up, devoured in the gaze of witness to raw,
powerful alive, responsive femaleness, and panther power.
I emerge, new
hear all now quiet
feel the shimmering beats remain and dew beads glowing
illuminating my illuminations,
a light never to be dimmed again.
I claw danced my way out of my cage.

Hollyhock Secrets

Pink and red Hollyhock stalks some 7 feet tall,
lit now greet the sun at first light,
they gently sway in the soft breeze.
Their secrets, hidden in those many buds yet to open.
They will not tolerate being brought indoors to adorn my table
and even though at risk of grasshopper decimation
they bloom from the center of their stalk,
they rise and descend like me. They remind me...
I too am blossoming from the center.
Both directions in my vertical ascension
and rooted now in my souls true earth.
They say you too dear one and remind me...
I have so many seeds left to offer.

Fox

Can't turn back.
No going home.
The Fox in me has been set free
to claw down the stars
to create galaxies
shape shifted,
now sporting my shiny fur and wildness
there is only the next galaxy I will create
each night.

Retrieval

I am retrieving myself piece by piece.
Why does the word piece look so wrong?
Maybe it's peace or should be peace. P E A C E
I am retrieving myself peace by peace.
I am ruling out all that is not that.

Now silence is a form of inner listening
rather than a type of punishment that strangles the voice of truth.
My peace is speaking, writing, hearing what is my truth
now and now and now
even if it is not peaceful.

Sometimes I even start to hear a whispered hopeful voice. Such
vulnerability to this wounded heart so exposed that one would likely
see the blood and scars of wishes not quite alive anymore partially
buried. My bare hearted confession that all is not OK now that I'd
like more, something better.

That peace is just over there...
Where...? Where hope is tucked under a garden pail
forbidden but piece by peace, ready to be revealed from my warrior
breast plate and armored heart, piece by peace
I will dig fiercely to uncover what is not at peace,

until a true equality, reverenced care rises
until this tender broken hearted feminine compassionate spirit
is retrieved. Until I am ready to speak hope to power
for a rising revered feminine.
Revealing intuition and care as strength and voice
for our sustained and nurtured earth, body, home
from now and for eternity

that's my piece and hoped for Peace.

Ahu Writings

the Inimitable Ahu Smith
multiple personalities sitting on a fence of electricity lines
www.ahusmith.com
IG - paintinhand

I spend my days searching for poetic composition. Search in my empty pockets. It finds me in the laughter of the wild children on the street. It captures me as I dance my body's beat of a new song. It chases me through colors on the graffiti walls of my neighborhood and abstracts me in broken English. It dreams at night and wakes me up. It surrounds me as I hear your whispers from last nights intimates. A brown-eyed Arabic glance, a wide-eyed Hayek-dressed woman. It blurts out lyrical rhythm in the song of the sweet little birds that visit me in the morning.

———————————

The inside of me knows you. Wants you to get to the fucking point. Wants your inspiration like a gun shooting its prey. I stand firm. I mean physically. I got the strong mental down, yet when certain times come, I fall. I wonder if I'll ever get back up. And when I do, over and over, I wonder why I wondered that in the first place. Inside me longs a feeling heard. Wisdom carried from the Universe through me. Orange geometry. Speckled flavors. Instincts precision. Tongue lapping, clapping, mapping. I lick the ashes. I plunge thoughts. I am the story. The greatest story ever told. Stories crowd my escalator. Jam my elevator. Push buttons off my blouse. If I wore blouses, that's what it would do. I like collars that stand up around my neck. I like pants with a wide waistband. Flowing legs draping along. I like skirts that allow the winds touch on my bare legs and ass. Sand. Velvet sand. Browns and rust. Turquoise and red. Yellow accents. White spaces. Black portals of thought. Put the greens in my pocket. The gold, the silver. Bronze eyes glow. Royal purple. Sky blue clouds. Faces and no names. My hair, long memories. I snip at it occasionally. I comb at night. Braid it like I honor my heritage. The water feels enlightened. It pours down my throat, nourishing my dreams. The sun. The moon. When I catch the rays, I pray.

———————————

My grandmother was the only person who didn't think I was an ugly baby. I consider her my real mother. Pee Maw Mama Kemp. Always got her to say this because she would purse her lips while saying it and spit laugh. PP..ing with the sound high at the end. Her smile matched her eyes. Mama Kemp was my mama's mama. Her maiden name was Cora Lee Stampf. She lived the same home throughout my life. I memory with this home.

Mama Kemp raised rosebushes, made homemade jams and jellies, and created art and writings. Once, I walked into the kitchen, and she was sitting over a metal pot, squeezing blackberries through a muslin cloth. The deep purple juice running over her hands and fingers. Her fingers long and spindly, her hands veiny and creased, knuckles slightly larger. Beautifully expressive. She wrote in cursive.

Once a year, her moonflower bloomed. She woke me in the middle of a full moon night. We sat together in her metal sliding couch-type chair and waited for this white flower to open in the moonlight. Her porch screened so one could see her gloriously large tree in the front yard. We rode buses together that picked us up by the coal mine at the end of her street. We traveled further downtown for shopping, stopping along the way, watching hippies mulling about their hippie house.

On some days the watering hose got loose from her hands as she watered her front yard. We laughed so hard as the hose whipped around like a snake as we made our arduous attempts to catch it. She seemed light and patient with me, deep and steadfast. A contrast from my mother, who felted pent up. Grandmother's laugh, infectious. Her yard, rows of plants and flowers, her side fence lined with roses. My first introduction to the smell of moist Georgia red clay was under her clay-carved basement designed for garden tools. I would sit inside and inhale the smell of deep, deep dirt. mmmmmm, my favorite smell.

She homed a parakeet in her side kitchen beside the refrigerator. The bird sang. First thing, every morning she would go to the refrigerator, sing with the bird, and drink a small glass bottle of Coca-Cola. Remember, Coca comes from Coca leaves. Yes, cocaine was present in Coca-Cola in her day. The original Coca-Cola factory, very near her house. She lived downtown Atlanta.

I would call her when feeling deeply sad, telling her that no one loved me. That my mama and daddy didn't love me. She always, always assured me that they did.

The corded phone between the bedrooms of her home on a cushioned bench, the bathroom next to it. She always put an iced water glass beside her bed at night. She told me, "Always keep your shoulders covered." "Don't wash your hair when you're bleeding." Grandmother, grandmother, she felt grand. Mama Kemp. Pee Maw Mama Kemp, that smile, the light in her eyes. Her writing desk. Those desks of strong, solid wood with the desk table that goes up and down. The small cabinets for pens and letter openers. I see her sitting, writing, and opening.

She created sparkling fans. She would paint little fans gold and design them with sequins and beads, adhere the fans to red velvet fabric, framing them in a gold frame, and give them away.

Grandmother. When she was put in a nursing home at ninety-three years old, I would visit her from New York City. Everyone told me she was "babbling." This babbling, a beautiful poem that I in turn spoke at her funeral. I titled it "Hurry," fore this word appeared often in her writing.

Her death, gentle. She simply curled in a fetus and stopped breathing. Before her last breath, I brought some blessed sand from the Karmapa, a Tibetan Buddhist monk, and sprinkled it on her head in the appropriate spot. I whispered words in her ear I learned from my Tibetan Buddhist study of Phowa, a meditation in conscious dying, for the soul to leave the top of the head. In Tibetan ways, they prefer the soul leaves out the top of the head for a better rebirth. Otherwise, it will find another orifice of the body to exit. I'm not sure if this played a part in her calm departure. I love thinking it did. When I read her so-called babbling, the beautiful poem at her funeral, everyone wept and was shocked that she wrote this piece. And further shocked by my attire. I dressed in a white conservative jacket with a short, tight black pencil skirt and high heels. I printed the poem on light blue paper with a photo of her in the right hand corner and distributed it to my family. It pictured her face gleaming with that beautiful smile and the light shining through her eyes.

I visited my birthplace for the last time in 1995, two years after her death, to honor my father's mother and my mother on Mother's Day. The day my mother did not recognize me for twenty minutes after being in her presence. And when she finally recognized me, she screamed.

_____

I sit in a circle with you all. The fire center glows from the crisscross logs burning. You dance. You sing. You cry. Wise women standing together, alone, Willow trees surround us. I rub blood on my face and dance your circle-sing. I am a thousand women growing a tree inside my forehead. The place of intuition and longing. You share. You care. You desire. You run. You stay. You are lost. You are Found. Bound by the truth of who you are in a drop of a moments minute. My tongue burns with silence. I'm washed. I'm clean. I roar. Wrapped in majesty of all women, men, children, animals, and reptiles. I see you in the sky like aliens who visit across stars and Planet O. Turn down the sheets so I may rest your knowledge, soaked in pleasure. Tackle the cost, burn the magic, and love my toes.

_____

(Burz/a) Agnieszka Brzezińska

– curious, shapeshifting being,
full of enthusiasm and playfulness
everyday mystic
busy with seeking beauty in all its countless forms
and loving dogs, adventure and books
shy artist

fellow traveller on the Red Path, where the erotic
and creative energy heals and guides us back home,
to ourselves and to the Divine

student at the Red School - Isis Temple

Into the Belly

I am inside the belly, floating in darkness. It feels strangely safe, strangely cozy. Like I can finally rest and let myself be held. The darkness is soothing, sweet, comforting. It nourishes me, it has everything I have ever needed. I am resting, letting go. I feel the sweet nourishing energy filling me in, deep down, to the bones. I am safe, held in that Great Cosmic Womb. I let that energy fill me up, fuel me, penetrate and permeate me. And slowly, ever so gently I can feel something deep inside of me uncoiling, unraveling. A wild creature. A gentle creature so soft, it does not have a name. For names hold a certain weight, a certain stiffness. And this soft wild creature made of dreams and love cannot be fixed into letters, cannot stay hidden behind a name. A soft, wild creature in a belly of a Wolf, in a belly of the Great Mother, ever changing, ever escaping definition. Not much of everything really, nothing and yet everything.

Being a witch is about following that annoying inner knowing, that little voice inside you that keeps gnawing at your bones. Little faces of fate. Little threads woven so completely you forgot how it started. There is no other reason to write than simply knowing that you need it. Nothing else can feed the soft wild creature inside you quite as well. No one else knows what can feed it. What is it allergic to? You simply cannot stop feeding it after it got a taste of meat of the story. You cannot stop after you learn what it means to be truly satisfied, to be where you were supposed to be all that time. You are at the destination and at the beginning at the same time. Simultaneously.

You keep feeding the creature word after word. It devours them happily. And yet it has already all of them inside of itself floating around. Which road through the forest will you choose? Your life depends on it and yet it doesn't matter. All of them are connected in a center woven together in a tight knot. Just let the darkness soften it. You can rest. You have arrived. Can you let the creature be?

Can you let it grow as it wants? Can you hold its infinite potential without making it smaller, bigger, more defined, shaped in some sense? Can you let go of ideas? And just let it be... Can you stand in the face of uncertainty and stand your ground? Not get offended by the vagueness? Stare into the void softy? Patiently? Feeding it breadcrumbs and cucumbers?

And maybe if you let it this wild creature will feed you back, will feed you with that special kind of truth of dreams and children. That truth that comes alive at night and in the forest. That truth we miss, we long for and that our longing makes our hearts hurt so badly, so badly we cannot let them be alive. So we numb our sweet soft heart. Because we cannot let ourselves hear that longing...

...And then one day, the time is ripe.
The time is now and you feel scared.
Fear is almost like another being
curled against your chest.
What is they won't like me?
What am I doing wrong?
You forgot little one,
It is only about being present in your own life.
Some people will like it,
some will run away scared.
You will feel scared.
But maybe it is just that.
Just building brick after brick.
Day after day. Nothing more spectacular than that.
Just building.
Just coming and watering the plants.
Just being steady,
being consistent.
Letting that soft wild creature in you
knows it matters.
It is the only thing that matters.

The Silence

There is a power in a women's silence that speaks louder than words. I learned it the hard way, I learned that slowly. Something inside of me was longing for silence, for solitude, for being alone, for being a recluse, a hermit. Living alone in the forest, close to nature. No people. No distraction. No other voice than mine. And yet you keep listening, keep listening, keep listening to random sounds. Your mind grows ears in the kind of silence and you start to listen to different kind of volumes, vibrations, sounds and voices. The world becomes symphony even if only inside your body. The music of your blood rushing to fulfill its duties, the everlasting rhythm of breathing in and out, the muscles contracting, the stomach growling. The energy in your body growing and circling, playing with your nerves, touching you, filling you with wanting . You are alone here. In your own capsule of silence. No one can enter. Who would you become? What will awaken within you in that loneliness? You. Your body. The grass beneath you and the sky above you. And wind touching you, always inviting. The leaves calling you in... The invitation.... The initiation... what will you choose? What are you dreaming about in the depth of your being? The time is passing and the seasons are changing.

Snow brings even more silence. Who would have thought? Silent night wrapped up in clouds and snow. Your greatest fear exposed here, lying naked and visible so clearly. Abandonment. Loneliness. Loneliness so painful your body hurts, so profound as if you were the last person on Earth, again the tiny human left alone crying for help that never came. Everyone leaves, everyone disappears. Disconnection, flight, freeze, your whole body in a scared panic. Lonely. Far away. Cold. Dark. Alone. No one comes. And yet you stayed. Here. And from the inside of pain, from the seed of trauma, you star to weave golden light of presence. Wave after wave. Bit by bit. You start weaving golden threads of different times, different dreams. Golden threads coming together of light, love, support, being loved, being seen, loving and seeing and being present and being connected, interwoven with other beings. And you stay inside the core of your pain like a spider inside her nest and keep creating threads with your body, the light coming out of your body like threads from the spider, the sticky threads that are connecting not catching, that are weaving new worlds into its being, bringing dreams to fill in shapes, inventing word to become body, the real palpable body of God. Here, inside you. God being born during silent night, God being born into you, into your body, the womb, the womb that creates sticky spider threads interweaving the web of connections, shining gems of light and dark, of sin and silent, of loneliness and togetherness until they all dissolve in silence.

The Voice

Zwinięty, ściśnięty, ból, zgubiony, niechciany, ból, ścisk, coraz mniejszy, coraz gęstszy, ścisk, samozapłon, ścisk, zwinięty, ściśnięty, ból, w kulkę, w kłębek, kłębek nerwów, zwinięty, ściśnięty, ból, nie ma miejsca, więcej miejsca, eksplozja, ryzyko wybuchu, zwinięty, ściśnięty, ból, głodny, zły, głodny, zła bestia, zwinięty, ściśnięty, ból, głodny, zły, bestia, kły, zwinięty, ściśnięty, ból, głodny, zły, bestia, kły, drży, zwinięty, ściśnięty, ból, drży, drży w posadach, fundament drży, ryzyko eksplozji, wybuch, buch, zwinięty, ściśnięty, ból, ryzyko eksplozji, wybuch, buch, głodna, bestia, zły, krew, krwawię, kły, kaganiec, uprząż, jarzmo, zwinięty, ściśnięty, ból, kaganiec, uzda, ból, jarzmo, uprząż, nie, krew, krwawię, kły, głodny, bestia, zły, bestia dzika, brzydka, zwinięty, ściśnięty, ból, kły, krwawię, zły, kaganiec, uprząż, ból, obroża, jarzmo, pług, głodny, zły, krwawe kły.

Wczoraj latałem. Tęsknię. Tęsknię za lataniem. Za niebem, za swobodą. Słowa obce. Rosną w paszczy. Słowa krzywe. Ja nie umiem w słowa. Jestem obcy. Nikt nikogo nigdzie. Język inny. Słowa obce. Bardziej kanciaste. Rosną w paszczy. Ja inny, zwinięty, mniej ściśnięty. Ból nie. Ja nie. Ja gdzie? Kły paszcza krew. Słowa jak kamienie w paszczy. Niewygodne. Umysł krzywy. Ja inne. Zwierzę nie. Ja. Inne. Nie zwierzę. Nie. Krzywe. Kły. Kły łamią się na słowach. Krzywe kły. Kły. Ja krzywe. Ja łamię kły. Ja kły. Ja nie. Ja nie. Zwierzę. Best-ia?

Where am I? Who am I? What was I doing? Where the time has gone? Lost... Not remembering... scared... full of scars... full of fear... sleepy... confused... learning life... so unpredicted... so crazy.... curl up and sleep... take your pills and calm down, baby... so scared... thin lines.... confined.... closed... confined closed.... for being too crazy... love where is love.... I cannot see the sky... the sky is falling.... confused... crazy.... confined... take your pills child.... learn to behave... don't pretend you don't know what is happening... confused... confined... where is the blue? What is my true? Confused... confined... take your pills child... where is the blue? Where is my true? Crazy... dizzy... sick... alone... confused... confined... take your pills child... where is my blue? Where is my true? Take your pills child... be kind...

Confusion... a lot of threads... Uncertainty... Lost? But found. The power of paradoxes. The tiny ball of fur wants to make sense... wants to hold onto something... wild ride... wild ride... wild... what does it mean to be wild? What does it mean to be wild? Wild... wild... wild... untamed... unhinged... forest... mud... wild... roaring in the forest... wild... sexual... what does it mean? Wild sexuality? Wild love? Wild Mercy? Wild fire? Wild feminine? Wild masculine? Can you love someone and leave ? Can you love someone and set them free? Set her free? Really set her free? Can you? Wild? Wild? Wild? Can you love someone and set her free? Wild? Wild? Wild? Crazy? What is crazy? What is wild? Where love become a confinement? Did I

put her in a cage? Where is my cage? Love...love..love … is a
golden light... Love is soft.. without fight... without armour... Love...
love her... love him.. love them... love us... love you... love me?
What is love? Is love a wildness? Is love a wildness? Where was
love? What was better? Where is the golden thread of love? What is
love?

Hungry.
Hungry.
Hungry.
Hungry hunter in the forest.
Who hunts Who?
Where is the Wolf?
Is the Wolf hungry?
Hunger, hungry hunger.

Pills of trash, you need to go through pills of trash. Hungry. Hunger.
Looking for. Searching. Foraging, Hunger. Dangerous. What will
happen when I feel my hunger? The king ate his babies. The king
made love with the maiden in her sleep. She slept through rape, she
slept through pregnancy, she slept through child-bearing. And the
only bad character is the Queen. What are you hungry for? Are you
afraid of your hunger? Are your afraid of the destructive power of
your hunger? Hunger... it ruins in your veins...it makes you who you
are.. it drives you... gives you purpose... and yet destroys... Predator
and prey... who eats you and what do you want to eat? Can you eat
your own babies? Can you eat your own tail? Hunger... is is what
makes us alive? What makes us want and long for and keep going,
keep looking for... Are you afraid of your hunger... Of the depth of it?
Are you? Yes, i am. I am scared shitless of my hunger. Of what it
will make me do. Of what I need, what I want Of destruction,
Corrosion. Compost. Scared. Death. Who eats death?

The circle... the circle of always.. to eat and be eaten... Food,
sustenance. Mother, milk... feeding babies.. from your breasts...

hungry beast. What will the beast in you do when it is hungry? How do you feed it?

I feel so tired... so stiff... so aching....
My body hurts, my jaw hurts.
Where is my creativity lost in the dark?
Do I give it voice?
Where is the voice?
How is there always a box, a box surrounding me,
a box shaping my voice, a box made of what I am used to.

I have been a thousand different women,
I have been a thousand different men,
I have been a thousand different beings.
I am looking into the corridor with so many doors.
It is dark. I feel like there is a thread
that I can catch and follow through
if only I would like to remember.
But today, today, it is so hard to remember,
I don't want that, I don't want to connect.
I hate my own shapeshifting,
wishing for simpler, more secure life.
And at the same time I am feeling guilty
for rejecting my gifts,
which caused me so much pain and suffering.
I want to be normal. I have too many facets,
too many dimensions. I am afraid I will be lost forever
and that no one would be able to hold me
to touch me. To receive all that I am.
So I keep closing the doors,
I keep hiding parts of me inside
with a lot of keys,
with a lot of effort.

I feel like my mind is a tangled web. The threads are screaming at me, pulling me in different energies, different scenarios. They want to be given space and a voice. So much time in the underworld. Squished, squeezed, hidden. Now they want to shine, they want to be seen, heard, to make noise, a whole rock concert. The voices in my head. The different stories, I was avoiding. The different stories, my life did not unfurl into.

Oh, why? Why? Why did I choose to mute you? The tending... the longing... the wild one... the masculine one... the other and the lover... the stories my life couldn't contain. I am a thousand different women and men, but only in my head... only deep down... hidden in my belly... And how my head is boiling and my body is on fire with that holy revolution... The voices inside of my head want a body, they want a body. Maybe it is my body or maybe they will steal yours... Maybe a wolf's body will do. They are ferocious. All that lives never lived... All that stories untold... Their time is now.. They are done waiting...There is no stopping them... no holding them back... nothing I can do...

They want their lives back, they want the sun on their skin and kisses on their foreheads and they want to make love to their destiny. Finally. Finally. I have a thousand hungry ghosts inside of me... And they are all wanting... wanting for tiny scraps of love… of freedom... of passion... of visibility... They want all of it... *Chcemy całego życia*... They want it all... No more bullshit... No more hiding... No more living on basic sustenance... We want it all and we want it now... So you see... I cannot sleep... they keep knocking... they keep calling me... they keep wanting me to feed them... my blood and flesh... the milk from my breasts... my crazy, unwanted babies... sweet monsters born from my soul fucking with my demons... The time of pretending is over... The time of being a good girl is over... Now a new time arises... A new sun is shining... a new voice reshaped and embodied... The choir of blood and horror and love and sweetness... my babies... I can finally let you breathe...

Gift Disguised as Curse

Fire, the fire that keeps burning inside my body, inside my skin. The inner knowing poking me – there is something else, there is something more... look for it... go and search... look for it... The erotic energy in my body that acts like a curious puppy, getting itself in trouble over and over. Why can't it settle? What is wild? Who really is a Wild Woman? Do you have to keep wondering? Ever wandering, not resting... feeling crazy... feeling misunderstood... feeling lonely... being exiled... Why do wild women keep being exiled? Where do I exile my Wild Woman? Where do I exile her? Fear her, scared of the mess she brings into my life. Untamed, unruly. Does the Wild Woman need to be exiled? Why? Who exiled her first? Did she chase herself out of the Garden, out of Eden, out of Paradise? Did God miss her? Call her back? Did she take her own rib and make an Eve out of it? Did she leave just a shell of herself, a past of her being? Similar enough to fool Adam, but robotic and zombie-like. Why did Lilith exile herself?

She needed to go. She felt she needed something else. She needed a different man, a different sex and she went to look for it. Why exile? Where was the exile? The falling from the sky? Why is she no longer present at the altar? Where is she when the God stays lonely on the monstrous, cold, golden altars in those stony buildings? Where is she hiding? Where did she go?

Ancestral story

Running... running... running... running through the woods... Fear... Running for my life... So fast... I cannot catch my breath... So fast so many times. Why don't I belong? What have I done wrong? Why don't I belong? Can I be here? They are warm. They have normal, warm houses, with families, and people. Connected. Surrounded. Understood. Witnessed. There is no one to witness me. Why was I exiled? What in me was exiled? What in me am I exiling? The sweet fairy? The mother? The one that thrives around people? The one that loves? Am I exiling my love? How much love is inside of me? How is love married to wildness? Why don't I believe I can have both? What is wild inside of me? What is wild? Where is my Wild Woman? What does she need? What is Wild and how can I feed it? Where is my Wildness? What does my Wild Woman need?

She needs a home, she needs a tribe, she need lovers that feel both safe and intimate. She needs to have children. She needs to write. She needs to have space. She needs beauty, she feeds on beauty. She needs dancing, dancing with other people. My Wild Woman needs home and tribe and lovers that feel safe and intimate. Lover? Lovers? She needs someone she can show all that she is, share all of her. My Wild Woman is soft, soft at heart, sweet and soft and loving, loves and receives love. She is soft and open and sees beauty. And she is surrounded by people that love her and cherish her and adore her and support her in every way they can.

My Wild Woman is surrounded by love and appreciation.

The whore in me

There is a part in me, that I hide, the part in me that is so sweet and open, so vulnerable and defenseless that I didn't know how to approach her. She got hurt time after time. And the world blamed her for everything and I learned to blame her for everything. The most tender loving part of me. The most sacred part of me. The holy whore in me. The one that sees beauty in so many people (oh, no, they taught, it can be only one person), the one that wants so badly to get on her knees to worship a dick with her whole being, the one who knows how to open her heart and legs before the Divine. The sweet loving essence of me. I am sorry. I am sorry. I didn't know, how to approach you, I am sorry I blamed you for all the pain I felt. When in reality you bring so much pain only because you know how to be soft and how to love.

Holy

Whore. Whole.
Whore. Holy.

I want to be your whore.
I want to give myself.
I want to suck dick on my knees.
I want to be seen
as I become the trembling mess of desire.
Finally unashamed.
Finally seen.

Devotion

To know
to will
to dare
to keep silent

What is the story of your devotion? What am I devoted to?

Devotion sounds so sweet, sweeter that commitment. Devotion sounds like love, like love-making, the making of love. Devotion, sweetness of love.

What is the story of my devotion?

Devotion means love, means sweetness, means deciding again and again. I want to devote myself to love, I want to devote myself to God and to discover my inner lover, my inner whore, my inner priestess.

What would she do?
What would my inner whore wear?
What is she looking for?

The part of me that knows how deeply sexuality and love are connected and intertwined, how in the depth they are the same.

Who am I? What do I need?
Can I let myself follow her calling, follow who I am?
Follow my love?

Follow my sweet opening, sweet devotion. Maybe to reach sweetness you need to agree to feel pain.

Love flows through you with full flavours of life.

COME CLOSER

BLIŻEJ

TAKE A CLOSER LOOK
LOOK
INSIDE
ME LOOK
CLOSER
COME

KUSZENIE

TEMPTING
TEMPTATION AT YOUR FINGERTIPS
COME CLOSER
WINGS
WHISPERS

SZEPT
TĘSKNOTA

MISSING
DESIRE
WINGS
COME CLOSER

BLIŻEJ

COME
AROUND
IN
CLOSER
COME
LOOK

LOOK
AROUND
IN CLOSER

BLIŻEJ
POPATRZ
BLIŻEJ

I know you want to.
Wiem, że tego chcesz.

Belonging

Be-longing
Longing to be
       to be seen
       to be understood
       to breathe
       to make sense
       to be allowed
       to live
       to be
       to be confirmed

Longing to belong. Belonging the greatest longing
De-longing. Be a longing. Become a longing.
Become a longing so completely there is nothing left.
Nothing separate. Just whole being of being a longing.
Whole being of belonging.
Whole being of longing
of belonging

Worship

I want to seduce you... to see how you open... how soft you can
become... I want to make you wet, so wet... I want to be all you can
think about, the next touch, the next sensation on your skin, the fire
inside and between us... I want to see you open and longing,
overwhelmed by desire, wild... I want to see you face when you drop
all the masks and pretending... when the only thing that stays is raw
pleasure... Beyond words, beyond imagination, beyond who you
thought you were... I want to see your naked soul and open it for you
so that you might get to know yourself... the raw, wet, pulsating,
unashamed you... I want to see how life moves thought you
unapologetically... how you become a wild river, untamed,
unstoppable...

Show me all that you are, all that you hide... I want all of you,
because I want to make love to all of you, each and every part of
you; the wild and the domesticated, the sweet and the roaring, the
curious and the virgin, the powerful and the soft... Show me all that
you are and then let me open you even further, even more... open to
more love flowing and multiplying between us... let me draw a map,
a sacred path on your skin with my tongue... traces of saliva... wet...
so wet... forgotten pilgrimage... let me worship at the altar of your
hips... and receive the sacred anointment... the holy sacrament of
your love... lets forget who we once were...dropping all the armour
till all we become is fierce frenzy of love and surrender and blurring
lines and openings and contractions... pulsating... the raw primordial
rhythms of love pulsating... life pulsating in the eternal rhythm...
relentlessly between your legs... between our hearts... between our
souls... till the edge between you and me and the world and God will
soften... will get lost in that frenzy... will blur in the pulse of life...

Let's go beyond what we thought is possible...

Dark Forest

Desire. Thick. All I can think about to fuck... to touch... That part of me deep in my belly. Full of desire. Dark like chocolate. Soft rich fabric. Flowing dark wine.Temptation.The devil. The horned one. The deviless. The lady devil. Lilith or Lucifer. Darkness incarnated. Fully fully embraced. Seduction. Fullness. Dark Eros. Dark desires. So dark like night. Feared avoided. Dark forest. Stuck in the dark forest. I wanna be your whore. I wanna give myself completely, give up all control, all power. I want you to do what you want with me. Touch me when and how you like. I want to be yours. Completely yours.Melting. I want to be your toy. Please, please let me give myself to you. Let me surrender totally. Let me give myself to you. Please, please...

I am begging you.

Beauty

She is so beautiful when she sleeps. Peaceful. Sweet. Undisturbed. Perfect. Her lips ready, but untouched. Her body soft, resting, humming with gathering energy, vibrating ever so slightly with the power she is not yet aware of. Blank page, clean canvas. Sleeping. Her beauty untouched. Pristine. Clean. Every cell beams with possibility. Everything possible, yet nothing done.

No road taken. No road abandoned. Just the smell of rich soil in the morning, just the soft sleeping cheek touching the mud. Oh... too late... she is waking... the mud touching her skin... the moss dancing with her hair... the moment is gone... the wind learning the shape of her body and her heart... whispering... into her ear.. wake up, Beauty... you are ready...

You are ready for the mess and the mud of this world.

sssssnake

I remember. I remember. I remember. Hissing. Low. The belly
massaging the Earth. Smell of mud. Low, lower. Near ground.
Hissing. I remember the snake-like movement. I remember
resonating with the Earth. I remember my skin on the ground, my
whole body on the ground. I remember shedding my skin layer after
layer in the loving embrace of Mother Earth. I remember the nights
spent as snake and the days tending to the well. I remember being a
priestess. I remember my whole body being an oracle, vibrating,
resonating with truth, oozing truth out with every breath. I
remember beauty and purity of shapeshifting. I remember being a
sacred snake caressing the Earth with my body, letting the holy water
guard me and guide me. I remember. The water on my body, the
water inside my body, dissolving, changing, touching, caressing.
The waves rocking me slowly. My body changing to embrace
eternal wisdom, to embrace infinity, my body guided by water to
embrace infinity, to embrace love and divinity to hold worlds inside.

Hot... sweaty... crazy... real... spontaneous... Keep going, they said...
Do not hesitate... Scared of change... of losing control... of appearing
crazy... sweet juice... sweet apple... Have you ever bitten an apple?
Juice on your skin following secret path... shhhh... shhhh... shhhh....
Don't ask don't tell.... shhh...shh...shhh... You cannot be seen.... for
snakes are a secret hiding in the bushes... shhhh.... shhhh.... shhhh...
moving slowly....kissing the Earth with every inch of your skin...
shhh.... shhhh....shhhh.... that is not allowed baby..... shhhh....
shhhh...shhhh.... don't move your hips.... shhhh....shhhh....shhhhh....
don't wear a red dress..... you might never come back..... shhhh....
shhhhh....shhhhh.... please....please....the box is so small.... It cannot
contain my whole writhing body.... I lost my way to Paradise....
Please... please... if there was a way out, there should be a way in....
please... please... I am lost... just the snake on the ground... where is
my destiny? Where are my wings? Missing... longing... heartache...
please...please... I know you cannot stand my vastness.... I tried to

shrink myself. I tried to be just one thing... just a woman... just a man... just a ssssnake.... just an apple... just an angel... What is an angel without his wings? Where do they go after I fell? Do the wings miss the fallen angels? Are there wings missing their snakes? Is skin missing the selkie? My skin - my wings? Are they the same thing? How many times do I need to lose them and find them? How many times? Until I finally learn.... They were never lost... My wing are always there... They cannot be taken just like my soul cannot be taken... They were there all along.

My wings were there with me when I bit the apple, when I let it travel through my body unravelling secret forbidden knowledge. My wings where there when I left Paradise... disguised as a snake... strangely divided... divided into man and woman... divided into below and above... into holy and sin.... My wings were there .... Wherever I go... They keep singing... They stubbornly refuse to leave.. No matter how many times I told them to... You see... You saw, what I did... Come on... You saw, who I am... You saw I am not an angel anymore... You saw?!?!? And still they stubbornly keep being stuck to my back.... as a visible and very annoying sign of Grace...

Longing

I am the longing... I am missing the impossible... I am.. I am... the longing... missing the sweet sound whisper of the ocean... ocean...ocean.. ocean... the waves waves waves... I hear the whispers... I wake up wet from the salty water... I wake up craving... and yet.. still nothing... nothing is happening... cannot find my way back into my own skin... believing that there is the only way... just that... believing I am powerless without my skin... that my whole oceanic being... my whole selkie heritage could be stolen.... that who

I am by blood and soul could be taken from me and used to hold me hostage... How could I believe such a lie... How could I forgot how my blood sings? How smooth is my breath under the water? How have I stopped trusting my own instincts, my own sisters calling me... How I let myself believe I am a trapped animal in this land cage.... Me, the rightful daughter of the ocean, the one that knows how to walk both ways... how to breathe here and there... destined to move gracefully between worlds... How could I believe my gifts can be stolen? How?

Breathe with your own green being

Secret life nourishing the soul. It is like bushes... starts small with a tiny seed. And maybe you just watered it a little. Maybe you gave it a little sun. And then it grows, and grows and grows and sometimes you tend to it and sometimes you just stand in amazement as the seedling becomes a plant and the plant becomes a whole bush and the bush becomes a forest. The forest becomes the jungle and all of a sudden your tiny secret life, your small acceptable opening into the wild is not so secret anymore. Because how do you hide a luscious, green, moist jungle inside of you? For God's sake girl, there are exotic birds singing and picking their fancy feathers. How do you think you can hide that melody coming from your belly? How do you hide the tiger growling inside of you? How do you hide the sweetness of a gazelle? How do you hide your own vastness, your own capacity to contain the world? After you let the jungle settle inside of you, there is no coming back.

There will be unexpected rainstorms, lion roars, monkeys laughing at your business partners and oh, honey, life was never sweeter... now you can finally breathe... breathe with your whole green being... breathe as you were supposed to... as one with the Earth... as a wildness that you are...

Advice from the fox

Slow down... slow down.. Let the wind play in your fur.
Do you even notice your fur? Let your paws touch the ground.
Swiftly, softly, steady. Do you even remember your paws?
The touch of grass and mud. When was the last time your paws
touched the mud? Slow down... slow down...Everything you will
ever need is already here. The sun, the grass, the food. When was
the last time you killed your own food? Let the blood fill your
nostrils and drip from your coat.

Thick... real scent...death is just another name for life.

My Beloved

My Beloved. Dark Eros with golden wings of love.
Let me worship you. Let me give myself to you.
A willing offering on your altar. Oh please. I need to surrender.

Whole-y
Holy.
Desire.

The sweetest religion.

My own shade of red

Red, red, everywhere red...

I am ready to claim my own shade of red,
I am ready to find my own voice and my own path.
I am ready to embrace my own shade of red.

The one I wear everyday
and I choose how sexy I am
and I choose how bloody I am
and I choose how wild I get
and how domesticated I can be.

For my own red thread is always there,
nothing can change it.

My own red has been my birthright since many lifetimes ago.
My unique shade woven together
by Power and Might
Softness and Love.

My unique thread woven by dragons and fiery snakes,
by priestesses and witches
and by home guardians,
by wisdom keepers,
by mothers and lovers,
daughters and sons.

My own shade of red,
that is inside me
and that clothes me from the outside
that runs through me and holds me,
that shapes my life and guides me.

Alchemy

The most sacred altar. The hidden truth.
You will carry into the world the keys.
The keys to alchemy. The keys to Paradise.
The more doors you open inside of you
the more space you hold inside,
the better you can lead people to themselves.
The light in the cracks.
You are the light that keeps shining through the cracks.
You are the beauty shining thought the cracks.
Joining. Connecting. Through shame.
Through forgotten doors and hidden pathways
you will find the way. The way from shame to sacred.

The Holy Whore.
The Priestess.
The Warrior.
The Innocent Child.
The Sweet Newborn.
The Shapeshifter.
The One that has many shapes and weaves them all in.
The Spider.
The Dragon.
The Lover.
The One that dances with shadows, dances with demons.
Demon Priestess.
The Witch, the Blood Witch.
The Heart Shaman.
The Father.
The Mother.

Now is the time

The time has come to finally become
the safe heaven for myself.
To be the safe nest for the little ones in me.
To be the lover I have always craved.
To give myself the life
I have always wanted.
The pleasure
that was my birthright.
The permission
I have been waiting for.
To breathe deeper
To live even more fully.
To be loved
and become love
fierce, devoted
delicious and sensual
love flowing through my body.
It is time.
It is finally time.
I am the one I was waiting for.

Trust

"I need to trust what was given to me if I am to trust anything."
—W.S. Merlin

The whore in me. The slutty slut
oh, how I wished she was different.
How I wished I was normal,
wanting normal things.
How I wished I was a nice girl,
a respectable woman.
And yet no matter how hard I tried
She is still here. The one that wants,
the one that desires,
the one that keeps turning my world around.
The one that didn't get the memo
about social norms, the one that is made of softness
and love and adoration and caress
and that holy trembling, that sweet anticipation.
The one that knows the way again and again
back to love. Oh, why I didn't trust her sooner?
I want to cherish her.
I want to bring her back
to her rightful place,
to ask her to be my guide,
my guide back to love,
back to divine love,
back to Paradise.
I want to worship her, to adore her,
to love her with all I got.
Thank you, thank you for never stopping
feeling, loving, becoming
devotion incarnated.

Alena Hrabčáková, MA, ATR
Licensed Art Therapist, Artist, Psychotherapy Specialist with
Diverse Adolescents and PTSD specialty.

Alenka, is based in Northern Minnesota and Northern Slovakia.
She has been an art therapist for over 35 years.
Her love and passions are painting and writing
since she was a little girl.
She has shown her work in America and in Slovakia
with hopes of expanding outward.
She has worked and lived on Red Lake Nation
on and off for 20 years
with her commitment to Ojibwa youth
and doing therapy from their traditional teachings.
She has also taught in Humenne, Slovakia.
She loves the old stories of her ancestry,
grandparents and parents all gone now.
But the images, symbols, landscapes and colors live on evermore.

She is an Adjunct Instructor
at The Center for Sacred Studies, CA. since 2012.
She has taught at The Ohio State University
and The Columbus College of Art Design in Columbus, Ohio.

THE WASTELAND

Wasteland is this vast space I do want to enter.
It knows my name calling me, nonetheless.
It is the one who peeks through the sidelines, putting up illusionary
borders, offering a temporal safety net.

I see you Red Fox, *Červený Líška*, out of my peripheral vision.
I wasted time, hours, minutes, years
on people, relationships,
amongst terrains under a terrible unbreakable spell.

Years have gone by flipping page after page
filling blank journal after journal.
Here goes an additional one with a cracked spine,
earthen amber to dust. Another narrative,
a cherished fable, *bájka,*
my ancestral lines twisted like wires on an open cage.
Many generations later it will be told or not.
Things resolved, or not.

I wonder why I walk through these swamps without my trusted
turquoise green rubber boots given to me by my beloved *Teta Anna.*

I can do this. *Dokážem to.*
No, I can't. *Nie, nemôžem.*
I can do this. *Dokážem to.*
No, I can't. *Nie, nemôžem.*
I can do this. *Dokážem to.*
No, I can't. *Nie, nemôžem.*

Spinning in the northern most tributaries of low-lying streams
of brilliant marina blue against towering rust colored grass.
I am conquering the unknown. Blowing winds
with no rhyme and reason. Ballads over Lake Bemidji.

I turn my ear to listen more intently. Missing a verse or two.
Wasteland follows me no matter far North I go.
North. North. Severne. Severne.
My compass only reads in this direction.
How far north do I need to go?
Do I need to go to Churchill, Canada with the diminishing polar
bears or further to the forsaken ice-scapes of ivory glaciers searching
for the long-toothed narwhals?
What would they tell me about the Wastelands?
Do I need to find the shamans and sleds
Can they save me if I cannot save myself?

Further, further I push myself to the precipice of the Arctic Circle.
Snow, ice, crevasses, till the white snow hare rabbits are invisible.
Cracking cracking crush crush the ice, ice cleats crisp crack.
Anchors thrown to my soul in this lonely somber beautiful
landscape.

"Where am I going?" I ask the driver navigating
in his seal lined furs.
I am not even cold.
The Wasteland shatters me or else I shatter it.
I am choosing the latter.
It is so difficult.
Pulling away the attachments.

Snowflakes freeze upon my mouth
making it hard to utter a word.

But what source of comfort would words serve me in this moment?

I need blinding silence with only the echoes of elements.

I can do this. *Dokážem to.*
I can do this. *Dokážem to.*

I HAVE BEEN A THOUSAND WOMEN

I have been transplanted time and time again in my personas of a thousand women. Here we go again, the new kid in school, you know the one with the bright red hair on the bus who has four good looking Slovak brothers, oh my two are twins, have you heard? No wonder every girl wanted to be my friend. A girl so shy and so quiet longing for friends, what will I face here? Sitting alone in the cafeteria can you relate to this desperate 14-year-old? Shutting down but saved by a paintbrush. Oh, I had my moments with popularity. Nominated for Homecoming time and time again. Never the Queen. That is okay.

I just wanted to be a Governess in my great grandfather's house. Freedom. Independent. Landowner. 10 hectares. Deep and passionately in love, repeat over and over so many colossal falls and lessons. Blissful bruising heartaches. Repeat. Intensity, runaway and hide. Tongue on tongue memorizing every ridge and bone. The integration of all these 1,000 women: Therapist, analyst, teacher, painter —churning always in the background. Landowner in her ancestral home. Let's stir the pot on the stove full of cabbage rolls permeating the air full of tomatoes robust cabbage, gobs of Hungarian paprika Never quite like *Bubka's*. The first thing I did once arriving, I ran through our cemetery full of wild orange and red poppies popping in every random place. Climbing the hills kissing my great-grandparent's tombstone and placing a painting I made for them of *Čierny Madonna*. Moss green patina stained with fading letters inscribed.

All of your thousands of women resting and nesting inside the womb of my mother and grandmother *Oh Matka, Oh Bubka.* My lineage of nesting dolls. Freedom and Abandonment One of the women inside of me loved to run and she would run and run. Unaware of the habitual conditioning of the grind culture. One must go almost feral to break the chains. I fell flat on my face time and time. Bruised eggplant purple soul. I rose again. Rising never in the way I thought I would. I fell in the carpet of green forest moss. Caressing my broken heart. Repairing. While I sipped on the stray raindrops on the fervent moss.

The only one whom can save these thousand women is myself.

Grabbing my journal, paintbrushes, pens. Toes touching last night's rainfall in my apple orchard bulging with delicate green and red striped apples. I attempt to gather them all. I was never able to do this until my fifties in my father's homeland village. Brown soil mud harvesting inside my cells. I had to know this was my home. This truly is my home and slowly. Slowly the thousands of women who are me, becoming me. Gathered in the cave of their structure.

A grotto filled with white and pale pink roses Homage to them all. Homage to myself. We finally made it home.

To my Dedko Jan Hrabčák, and my father John Hrabčák. To my beautiful Karas family in Slovakia. To my graceful and beautiful mother, Audrey who made me always feel contained in love. To my beloved brothers, Greg, Scott, Mark and Micheal Hrabčák, so many endless loving and fun memories that live on eternally. To so many beautiful teachers, and close friends whom I will thank personally.

THE HOLDER OF THE BLUE STORIES:
Držiteľ Modrých Príbehov

There is an ache inside of me. *Bolestivé.*
The ache how can I describe it oh beholder of the blue stories?
The ache to paint it out. I paint hour upon hour
lost in the crescendo of the moment, minutes, hours.
Paint and brushes stacked with endless colors,
cerulean, yellow brilliant summer,
 red oxide, burly wool browns,
turquoise blue, pale portrait pink.
Pens line my studio all in careful arrangements,
fountain inks amongst bold mars black.
Faithful paper ready for the cascading symbols and images
I ache terribly for you to get out and fly, be released.
I ache terribly for you to know me
and help me to know myself better.

Through thousands of colors
Through thousands of words
Through thousands of unknown collective unconscious images

Buzzing like a swarm of anxious bees released, frantically.
Bees in the belly. I unzip myself exposing my earthen skin.
Completely exposed in this minuscule moment.
Will the bees catch the symbols, the words,
the heartaches, the sorrow, the beauty, the bliss, the melancholy
and help me transform this massive canvas
of my infinitesimal being?

Words, images spin like a carousel of painted horses
in the dimmed reservation night.

World of paint, letters, unknown languages
never uttered till now

Nothing makes sense in the narrative now. Lost.
Stratený Gloriously lost. *Slávne stratený.*
I ache for you to understand me.
This intrinsic marriage to words, paint,
colors, tones, hues, shadows.
I ache to understand you.
Sisters and brothers,
I believe this is why we are all here right now.
No coincidence you are reading these sentences.
Our hearts are aching, craving longing for this
acknowledgement. Close your eyes.

Not too fast.
Slowly. *Pomaly.*

The moment has arrived.

To all my Red Lake Nation Students in Northern Minnesota. I see
you. I acknowledge you. I love you. I also acknowledge you dear
reader. Art is medicine and healer; I can promise you that.

Starý Starý OLD OLD PLACES

Let's go to the *starý starý* old old places
Here is where I am deep in the thickets.
Picture a baby blue periwinkle clean fresh lake
Standing at the edges of Lake Bemidji
Ojibwa word meaning when a river crosses a lake
Mississippi and Bemidji
It's a bit like two entities in nonlinear space

Liminal

Life is a dream a bodhisattva told me recently in a dream.
Paint it at the foot of the bed on the wall.
Make a mural to remember it.
I will take note of that sentence all this time later.
I am at the reeds that tenderly sway in
along the lake containing wild rice
It is glorious.

To be this age and having the 18, 21, 23, 30, 40, 48, 50, 55
and 60-year-old, together with me facing the lake.
I am all these ages.
A Goddess for each age, year, decade.
It is a mystery.
A web, I have spun over and over,
using my Bubka's embroidery scissors.
In the thickets are landscapes
that changed my life forever
too numerous to name.

The Monongahela River, The Ohio River, Gull Lake, Lake Michigan,
Hoover Dam, Lake Bemidji, Red Lake, The Pacific Ocean,
silt and soil, dams. Swimming.
Memories like water spirits swim by.
Too briefly and sometimes too long.
Lake *Eva Domasa* in Slovakia.

Circumambulation.
Water, waves, tides flow up and down all around
In the night sky
In the *starý*, old places.

When the curse of silence can no longer be your framework.
Curse of silence
You have served me many years protecting me,
building walls and barriers for others not to be able to climb
You no longer serve me.
I release you from my betrothed asylum.
Key thrown into the raging sea.

A rabbit fur of many layers of cinnamon
and white wrapped in all its beauty
falls at my feet at Trinidad Beach.

Rip it up
Rip it up I say
Now.
I unzip my mouth.
I release all the gauze and bandages.
I give myself CPR
No more
No more.
No more.

I release you from this melancholy dance of rain and silence.
No longer betrothed.
Gone. Gone.
Preč. Curse of silence
when my words needed to be spoken.

Ready to release the thousands of syllables
like uncaged doves.

MY DAY IS SPENT SEARCHING FOR STORIES

Hansel, Gretel
I pick up the fallen crumbs.
I watch the birds communicate in sonnets and ballads.
Red winged blackbirds, red headed woodpeckers,
pale blue nuthatches, effervescent grackles
I have learned the tenacity of the fearless chipmunk.
I follow the nuthatches first to arrive and the last to leave.
The squirrels that stuff their cheeks for a banquet later in time.
Sometimes it is good, sometimes it is best to bury it.
I watch the mothers and fathers feed each other and their babies.

I follow the crumbs of conversations at the local farmers
amongst hot crusty old world sourdough breads, plumb zucchini,
minuscule cherry tomatoes, bursting green dill, curly kales.
I carefully place them in my homemade woven basket

Tenderly made.

Teaching me about compassion, irresistible gossip, the conversations
that I really should not be listening to, but I cannot help indulging.
Heartbeat Heartbeat

I follow each nuance as a symbolic riddle.
A message wrapped in a slender scarlet ribbon

The story is crumbling
This crumbling narrative
as I try and catch them into my cedar basket.
The words come to at the wee night hours
when the world is in their slumber

I can think clearer
I awaken to write till the words tumble
Stitching dreams stitch upon stitch
like uncaged flying doves.

THE FOX SERIES

PART ONE
Fox Fox
Liška Liška
Can I ever go home? I want to go home.
I want to stay. Life, life, death.
Fox Fox
Líška Líška
Can you help me find my way home?

PART TWO
Red fox lies exposed under my bedroom window the night before
someone I loved died. Red fox lies under my bed, shy elusive
tending to my savage wounds, begging me to get out of bed.

I try, I try again, once more. The red fox shakes me, yet I collapse
once more. I am not ready. Dreamworld takes me on another route,
on the neon ochre tour bus to somewhere close to my lips. I hear the
whisper stating I am in the Shetland Islands, Scotland. Giving me
images of my maternal grandfather's homeland. I tell Red Fox this
life makes no sense anymore. Papa said to my little soul of self at
seven, hell is on Earth. What once was or all I believed is shattered
with irreplaceable glass. No longer manufactured.

Red Fox tells me to write a new book. I have hundreds of miles of
journals, every home, every place. Where to begin? Diatribes
unburied. The Red Fox climbs into my favorite orange poppy
blanket, the one I have carried for years for comfort. It snuggles
beside me telling me to trust even though I feel I don't have an ounce
to give. They lay their head on my belly as if was comforting a late
term pregnancy, all the cries, labor, moans, tears descending
downwards to the womb. Releasing the placenta, the child of my
art. I tell them this does not make sense. No answers. I sink further
into ease caressing its coarse soft red oxide fur.

We speak in a language with no words conveyed. The silence that anoints your check with a kiss banishing all fears. I sleep like a newborn for hours, days, minutes. The spell has been broken. I am with you. You are with me. Evermore. Evermore.

PART THREE
Fox pelt
Left on the bed today
Brazen reds cool oranges
Magical
My outlier Spirit Guide
I need your strength more than ever.

PART FOUR
Red Fox scratches me on the forearm this morning. Waking up I have another teaching I hear in my mind's eye. I am blurry eyed, no medium roast coffee yet. Red Fox wants me to go outside. Hurry. I get up with a stale mouth with my midnight black Standard Poodle Romeo. Kaleidoscope images spin in my yard. Spin spin spinning. Cedar tree to Oak to Pine. Wild bluebells with ivory white queens Anne's lace. Look look chipmunk comes closer. Baby squirrel no longer is afraid of us. Dewy moist budding green grass. Neon moss growing on yellow oxide bricks. I grab my journal. It tells me I cannot proceed further till I give gratitude. I gathered my gifted cedar from Red Lake Nation. I listen. I write down my list of teachers no matter how many. I will thank each one of them in this moment. A deep respectful bow. Thank you. Over and over. Bow to the magnificence of dreams. Bow to the teachers. Swirling. A random Sunday of Red Fox Teachings.

PART FIVE
The birds are singing me home. Every blackbird. My morning nuthatches greet me enthusiastically. Squirrel meanders down the tree. Curious. Chipmunk grabs a random black oil sunflower seed. Mating pileated woodpeckers. Glorious oh glory moment. Pause pause. Pozastavit' pauzu.

Radical stop and pause. They know me. I know them. Tip toeing
closer. Red fox the outlier.Hiding behind the wild lilac brush,
bramble, branches. I see it. It sees me. No coincidences. My pen in
motion. Like simmering chicken potato soup bubbling on Bubka's
gas stove from the 1960's. Aluminum timer set for 28 minutes. I
hear you. I hear you. I see you. I see you. I acknowledge you. I
acknowledge you.

Fox prints left in the soot and soil.

WHERE DO THE STORIES HIDE?

Where do the stories hide?
I feel they hide in my *duša*, my soul.
Duša is my hidden interior castle.
My cavern of secrets. My private domain.
I have built up so much grout, stone, pebbles, mud
It is endless. Push push push away, tear down
Then my lungs collapsed last year, breathing was more complicated
I was hanging by the limbs of my branches leading to my breath
The branches were vanishing. I had to stop.
There was no other choice.

Like a mole, a prairie dog I had to burrow.
Building intricate tunnels.
Going every which way to find out the truth.
I exhausted myself. Tattered.
Breath breath breathing more difficult.
I fell in the Shinto of my *duša*.
I laid down on my gathered Ancestors bones
Cradling them. Cradling, crunching them till then joined mine.
Torn threads, garments, stitches as big as Lake *Eva Domasa*
near my village *chata*.

I had to swim through my tears.
Mile after mile. Exhausted. Invigorated.
My heart was pumping overtime and the stories cascading with no
reserve. I rested into *Bubka's* crocheted blankets of deep blues
hour upon hour. Blessed Communion
Now it is time to begin,
I have received the Host.
I was asked are you ready
I replied, *Áno Áno Áno*
Yes Yes Yes.
A spindle of *rusa* red rose fell at my feet.
Áno Let's begin here.
Do not skip any details.

*For all whom what to write, my father always said, "If not now,
when?"*

TAPESTRY OF SPINDLES

I am the pile of discarded spindles
Those beautiful wooden spools
Full of every color one could ever imagine.
Imagine rich ochre, Indian summer yellow, poppy orange, emerald,
green, bursting purple, robin's egg blue,
plum jam and eggplants, opaque pink.
Here we sit in piles of pins, pincushions, embroidery threads.
No one knows we are here.
In a wayward village of Bubka's village in Slovakia
An abandoned church burned to the ground
but the foundation that she went to in secretive rosary circles.
Mary, Mary Full of Grace.

We sit in the burned down remnants of the nave
by a war we will not mention.
More unspoken stories.
Cold neglected unattended
except for the poppies and wild daisies
between the cracks and crevices.
The threads longing to be spun
into glorious capes, shawls, blankets,
newborn clothes, capes, heirlooms in a cedar chest.

How did we spend our hours and days you asked?
Imagining our new owners finding us
creating these designs amongst the shimmering starry night.
One day that girl in the red cape, Alenka, found us.
I thought she was from another story,
but she came unannounced.
Imagine our surprise? They all coalesce, don't they?
Alenka had an oversized wooden picnic basket
arriving with ooohs and ahhhs.
Laughing with a large toothy smile, dancing.
She asked for permission for threads.
Could they go home with her?
Could she return them to their rightful owners?
The spindles cried and cried and cheered and wept.
Yes, they wanted to return home.
Alenka left sage, cedar, juniper berries
to their temporary *dusa.*
Skipping with a slight hop.

Have no fear.
I found the treasures again.

To the most beautiful seamstress, my mother Audrey.

THE LOST GIRL TRIBES

I am in the *kmeň* the tribe. The Lost Girl Tribe. Stratené Dievčatá
I suppose I have inklings of this since age 12, 14, 15, 28, 38, 40, 50,
to now 60's. *Terza,* Now.

I love the lost girls. I have been an art therapist for adolescents for so
many years now, helping the outliers and the misunderstood. The
un-listened to. I am one of them. Once. Twice. Even now.
How did I get so *stratený?*

I suppose it is hard to say when I did not fit in the *príbehy,*
the stories. I love the *starý starý* old old stories. One's that *včela,* the
bee stings in your body, you itch to calm the raging skin. The ones
that stuck an arrow in your heart.

I love{d} the ones who were invisibly bruised, the empaths, the
sensitives, the misfits, street smart, *Cigáni,* Gypsies, the bad girls,
the bad boys, because we all hold some of this there by something
greater than us.

I wanted to unravel their stories. Pull them apart like an *orol,* eagle.
Pry them open, talons dug in for the catch. Pry the *kosti,* the bones
The guts devour the story. Can you devour a story?
Áno Áno Áno Yes Yes Yes

I am a lost girl with my bright red tomato cape on. Chunky, clunky
bangles and tangles. I want to dive into the plot. Sew into your *duša*
Never to be ripped out. Forming your *telo,* your body, into you. Into
me.

I one of the *Stratené Dievčatá* -the Lost Girls
Embroidered on my puffy white periwinkle blue sleeves

Evermore.

THE FOX ON THE ROAD TO LAKE *EVA DOMASA*
Afterthought. 7/31/24

The fox pelt blazing orange red sits on my morning lap
A reminder claiming… yes, this experience really happened.
It arrived like an unexpected stork delivering a new baby girl
on my mint green porch. It came with the name Sophia Audrey.
Dedicated it to your future prodigy.
I have only met her in lucid dreamscapes.
The Village I live in already knows.
Am I surprised? News carries faster here than airmail.
You know the American woman, Alenka Hrabčáková
living in her Ancestral house?
There is no need for an announcement.
From Giglovce to Nizna Sitnica to Pritulany?
The mailwoman told everyone.

I drive down the highway to Lake Eva Domasa and see a freshly
deceased fox. I cover it in a blanket from my truck and place wild
yellow daisies and tomato red poppies at its feet. I weep.
The culmination of this journey. It is finished.
Birth and death all in one day.

The bells toll it is 5:55 PM the local Catholic Church releases the
tones of Our Lady of Sorrows in higher octaves. The hour of my
mother's death. Sorrow and Beauty. A book is born on my Ancestors
back and soil. I can't wait to visit my relatives hoping we will
celebrate with much vodka, laughter and cheer. The circle continues
and I cannot wait to see the next rising star in our lineage. I will wait
years, hundreds, thousands. I do not care. Because I know all of this
is an old *starý* story. A narrative woven on the earth, ground, mud.
Prayed over with repetition more times than I can count, with
wayward buried rosaries. It is done.

It will be done.

Kyla Dawn

kyla lives in northern california
with her little dragon pup chihuahua dracarys.

she has been teaching people how to find their breath,
being and magic in their bodies for over 20 years.

she has been collecting stories her whole life
and is now finding so much joy
in watching them dance out onto paper.

a huntress of golden truth threads
and a multi-dimensional weaver of worlds,
kyla is here for the great liberation
and blossoming of love.

the job

some journeys you set out on don't have a clean tidy ending
they did not go as planned and they went exactly as planned
sometimes you just have to decide this is the end
it is time to wrap it up and be done
done waiting for life to do it for you
sometimes it is time to say job well done
well the job is done anyways
in all the ways the job got done
the job could keep being done... and done well
but sometimes it is the time, like now,
to just let the job be done
no more struggle about doing the job
differently, better, more, when, where
no more doing more of what is already done
sometimes the journey, the job, the seeking, the exploration
simply needs a punctuation
a final expiration
not from life and not from anyone else
sometimes like a time such as now
it is time for you to place the punctuation
at the end of the story that is done
it it done
the job is done
a job well done
it is done
the end
PERIOD

skin

too wild to be claimed
oh how I ache to be taken
but they always go
or i slip away back into my skin again
too wild to stay long enough to grow
a child of my own
they always go
or i slip away back into my skin again
slip sliding this way or that
deeper diving, higher flying
they call it freedom
such a free spirit you are
is this freedom?
always coming or going,
not knowing who's skin i am in?
is this freedom?
they see it that way
free spirit, wild, untamed
slipping in and out of deeper higher
still the ache to be claimed remains

fox lady

fox pelts, lingering stench
for days, weeks, months, years, lifetimes
i miss you
please come back
or keep running
whatever sets your soul free
and has you alive
feeling full of all the life
me, i died that day you left
but that's ok i'll die 1000 times more for you
i killed us
i'm sorry, please forgive me
i love you
i see it now
your smelly magical wild too muchness
please come back
and slap me in the face again and again for eternity
with your unacceptable disgusting decaying fur
i want it
i want you
ALL of you

get back here you stinky,
kinky,
foxy
witch

goddess bless the lover who comes from no mind.
a grab, a gaze, a caress, a squeeze informed by this only now
moment.
no thought a match for the magnetism of breath penetrating flesh...
dancing through whole body come alive.
not even the latest hot sex tip, tool, book or porn shot
can pierce this lover's devotion to what is true.
awake, aware, eyes wide shut and open it does not matter

for presence is the teacher now.
true to the moment is all there is and he knows it.
he knows his true power lies in this one sacred breath,
poised for grace, ready for action, listening for god
traveling by air..
inhale...
guiding his next move,
exhale...
until there is no more guidance,
there is no separation...

doing, undoing, stillness, motion, push, pull, flesh, spirit, breath,
body,
man and woman all become one
as this holy moment of truth...and beauty...
one breath...one dance...
yes... he has found his church,
his place of worship,
his source of inspiration for all of life,
this breath is his everything...
and to share it with her.

they call it heaven on earth.

picasso face

freshly showered, yet still sweat dripping
in my favorite leopard print top
i walk down the steps from the hot yoga republic
to your confused smiling face
where are you going? i thought you were teaching.
suddenly my face melts into a swirling picasso painting
my stomach leaps into my throat or my heart jumps
deep into my guts
i can't quite make out this roller coaster ride inside.
i want so badly for you to kiss my lips
and help me locate my body parts again
put me back together, why do i fall apart inside when you are near?
i take off my matching leopard print hat, roll out my yoga mat
on the concrete parking lot and lay down flat,
limbs outstretched wide in the sunshine.
from the outside it may look like sweet surrender, but on the inside
i am seething with 1000 snakes desiring their next meal
will you come out and say hi before class like you said you would?
what will you say, what will i say, how will it feel, what am i
doing???
i am sweating more now
than inside that 105 degree hot pilates class.
the sun is beaming straight down from the bright blue sky
and i have no where to hide.
what am i waiting for? you're not coming out or maybe you are
but still…what in the actual fuck town am i doing?
oh yeah chocolate cold brew, that's where i was going.
i roll up my mat almost making it back to my car
without turning around
i want to see your face picasso for me like mine does for you
please don't come out now. i have made up my mind,
i'm out, i am going.

i am slithering my sweaty body away from this hot hell fire
i find the air filling my lungs again,
and i remember to breathe
gripping the steering wheel i drive away back in control
thank god you didn't come out and see me star fished on the ground
dead to all ambitions and desires except for your picasso face
swirling into mine
blue yellow broken shards of brown red and pink shedding skins
cold air blasting from the air conditioner
take me from this burning pit of desire
i'm all about ice cubes and cold coffee on my lips now
this is all i need.

dragon mother

when fire speaks she may begin as a spark, a flirt, a crackle,
her hunger grows, she feeds and expands until she is the very force
of transformation,
and when she comes ripping up from the core of the earth herself,
roaring through your flesh like a dragon mother
protecting all of creation
there is no hiding from this ... of fire
there is no separation from this power
she is you, she has your body now and demands you stand up
rise like the phoenix from the ashes
this fire has been burning since before time
and her time is now time to burn, burn bright shine a light
on all that is true, devour all that is not
only what serves love now
the dragon mother has returned
and she has a dance, a fire trance to dance

water woman

i can't stop crying
the tears keep falling
dripping drop down my face
where does all of this water come from
why does it keep falling out the corners of my eyes
what does it want from me
and where is it going
falling down down down
i fall with the tears
into a dark well
i am not alone here
there are others
hiding from the danger above
is it safe down here in the depths of the dark
why do we hide women in these deep waters
oh yes the throbbing pain of the knives
they keep throwing towards our spines
the cool waters of the well offers relief
so this is our life now
just sitting here hiding in the dark
this is how we live now. is this living?
a tear drop falls into the still water
turning it from smooth to ripples
circles circling more circles
rings ringing out and out and out
how beautiful the water dances
when she receives a single tear
i wonder how she will respond
if we sing her a song
a lick of their wet lips
the women open their mouths
and out comes the grief song
wails of ooohs and ahhhs

oooh this is our grief song ahhh
no more will the pain live on
it is time we learn the truth of our song
it is time we learn the truth of our voice
it is time we learn the truth of our truth
there is an ache inside
an ache to grow
to expand, to express, to love
an ache inside of me that is not known
and wants to be
wants to come out and dance in the light
just like the water danced with the tear drop
i can dance with these tears
the ache, the tears, the dance are all inside of me
and they have a story to tell
now how to get out of this well
i cup my hands take some water and drink
one long smooth sip to my lips
i turn to rainbow tunnels inside
following waters way
through iridescent rivers, lakes, valleys, streams
deep into wells and layers of earth
up through yoni shaped clouds
of colors from another world
oceanic sparkles that tickle
through erotic bodies alive squirting juice
purple, pink, orange, gold and blue
the holy fountain of youth
the water dance is pure magick
pure life. pure living
in connection with all there is
so cry woman, release
bleed, cum, sing, swim, dance, lick
release your water
you are pure magick

ice queen

i am so cold
i light some frankincense
and watch the smoke roll around in the air
inviting it's warmth inside me
how many hot coffees and teas will it take
to warm these inhospitable bones
please…
i gaze outside at the bright light from the sun pouring down
it looks warm but i know the air is crisp and still
from yesterday's storm
how many hot yoga sweats will it take
to melt the frozen stories inside
melt them out of me
turn this icy ache into fluid fairy tales flying alive sprinkling magick
and medicine for all
who have the eyes to hear and the ears to see
perhaps i can start w an ice pick
carving out the shapes that have shaped me
i am so fucking cold
just call me the ice queen and fuck off

the invitation

i am so tired
so utterly fucking exhausted
i am shaky inside,
the process they say to trust has me
feeling so numb... and dumb
what will have me come alive?
i don't know but this coffee
may be the actual death of me
how do you survive the lightening storm inside?
magenta hot lava orange burning
ultra red crayon crackles
of fiery colors ripping apart my insides
how do you surrender to this blazing storm
...when... you... are... her...
And then it arrived
it was unexpected
the invitation to exhale
so i let myself fall apart
with nothing left but the words
trust love
i sink to my knees and ask for guidance
my lungs are filled with liquid crystal
and i am taught how to breathe again
with mud and tears I begin to rebuild myself
from the gaze of the earth and sky
listening... opening... feeling for truth
i find a deep devotion to this new/ancient way
in full surrender i learn to dance
to dance with this moment
every move born of love
fuck it, love it...time to trust love and only love...

home

if this is home, i want to be forever lost
an orphan to the stars
i can't breathe
listen to me
hugs that feel like a dagger in the back
black tube snaked around my torso tightens
as my shoulders crawl to my ears
adhd i have to pee
melted goo
if you only knew
fuck being nice
i want it real
knotted thoughts
tangled torcher
battered bodies
bickering birds
this land is suffocating
so much is buried
under here
covered bridges
covered dreams
ancient cries ancient eyes
stuck in the mud
masks for days
it is not fine
nothing is fine here
hardened necks
tortoise shells for backs
spineless business
busyness stop
listen to the whispers
chiming in the wind
there must be love here

buried deep in this land
there must be love here somewhere
dig deeper sink swim
surrender the stories
are waiting to be uncovered
opened and written again
come home, the real home, come home
…
owl cackles
gar splashes
too hot to fish
the hummingbird
wraps her tiny feet around my finger
sipping nectar
pain in the neck
pink tipped nails
clawing for the kink
rip it out
GET OUT!
nowhere to go
there used to be a heaven inside
i've been there
where did it go?
ask a better question
how did i get there?
shhh…ride a breath
so soft, follow the thread
sparkling ever so slightly with iridescence
through thick sticky cob web spells
straight into the taboo herself
they don't tell you the gateway to heaven
is an endless black hole of heartbreak and pain
pull out the dagger and slice open the portal
step inside it's blinding light
come home, the real home, come home

it's good

oh when it's good, it's good
touch me…yes just like that, you have my attention
go ahead touch me… now touch me until you love me
give me gifts if that makes you happy
just don't stop caressing my body
explore every crevice of my holy terrain

tell me your secrets
the ones that live deep down, the dark well within
locked off to the world kept so preciously hidden
i am mesmerized by the words you are not saying
swimming in your soul waves is my place of worship
i take a deeper dive into these holy waters
my exhale expands and you feel so seen
and heard and haven't uttered a word in hours
and what would you like from me?
my magical presence of course

say no more i know just me being by your side lights up your world
and has you feeling tingling alive all over inside
all 37 trillions cells you say
every one refreshed, renewed with eros herself
mmm i take a breath sinking deeper into my pelvis
down into the earth and back up again
my heart, expand my energy glowing every cell awake
i am whole, fluid body alive and well, we are
i take a walk into the coffee shop
oh i love your shoes
sparkly magenta waves dance from my lips
seducing the barista with one whiff
she lights up beaming her nectar du jour
filling up the entire shop with swirls of lilac and lavender
a true potion #9

a collective breath of pure erotic pleasure
this is living magic
can you just be yourself already!
rise as the rose
i am ready
thank you thank you thank you
i drop down into my feet and back body a little more
opening wider she blooms
alright who's next, who wants it
the magic fluff, the love puff, the good stuff
this is how we love, this is how we fly
before we die damnit
cuz when it's good, it's so fucking good

sleeping beauty

gah… ouch… ah!
that hurts. these thorns are sharp
blood dripping, drop
where is my way in
to the beauty caught in a deep slumber
under a spell. i can spell
where is my way in
my way in to her
here? there?
now? never?
next? time…100 years you say
how did he make it through this dark thorny death trap
a lethal barricade to the only thing worth dying for
living for, are we living or dying
blackout tie took me out
for a moment i fell into a deep sleep but just for that part
he made it in and i awaken again
the way in, following the breath,
feeling my way in, eyes turned in
thorns wrapped around my lungs
how to get in? i'm stuck in a spiraling tunnel
broken glass shards all around
ouch blood dripping, drop
perhaps i'll just die here
hear…shhh…listen…hear
here here, there there
how to get from here to there
the air, breathe… the air…ride…or die…
how can i breath when i am choking on my own damn blood
breathe breathe breathe again and again,
let it in, let her in
let her in
let us begin again

seaweed spine

say something…anything… say something…
reaching out to a dead ends known
it's so dry here in this lonely place,
crackles of once connected circuits of dripping nectar
i call back my opalescent tendrils
wrap around my twisted spine
bathing my parched body
drinking in the nourishment of her presence now
golden thread of truth awaken
breath hydrating cells
fluid body come alive
how quickly the sleeping undulation unwinds
the serpent dance up the spine
seaweed breathing presence gate
a key hole so tiny
breathe through the slime
the eye of the needle
a still point in the ocean,
i've never been here before now
but i've been here 100 million years
this point waiting to be explored
she needs a drop of this golden nectar
just a drop
just one sparkling drop
and look at her begin to bloom
fuck a drop
give it to her
give it ALL to her
how long has she been waiting for this
she only wants to bloom
she wants to be adored
but mostly felt
to know herself

eyes closed
will you look now
eyes closed wider
look again
look closer
look with your breathing seaweed spine

burnt lips

exhale
i fall into your arms
inhale
we fly through golden sequin trees
exhale
spaciousness
inhale
a purple pyramid from deep within consciousness
your burnt lips on mine
sends tingles down my spine this time
'come on let's go the bedroom, we are magick'
you pick me up and gently toss me onto the bed
our bodies bounce in erotic bliss
i took one look and knew
'i prayed for your cock to be just like this!'
i'm so glad you came over for lip and brain healing
i know this place
where the stairway to heaven takes us

right into the forgotten
truth…
we remember
sun rays of infinite light
from lifetimes of coming apart
we fall together again
scent of home in the air
no more searching
wandering lost
we've been here all along
home is exhaling
with you
honey on my tongue
don't go, you're gone
you left
and i call you smart
but you're right here
i feel you
feeling me
constantly i feel
a bee buzzing buzzz
on my tongue
on you
turns shock waves overwhelm
exhale
melt
home is here in the now
we melt
can we climb the stairway to magick in the purple pyramid again?
i remember this place
thank goddess you can handle snakes
the serpent is awake
and she knows the way
home

you feel me too much

please don't stop talking
because if you stop then there is space for me
and you feel me too much
i feel you feeling all of me and that's not fair
i'm squirming in my restless body
what do i feel?

lifetimes of pain wanting to break me open
into a thousand tiny pieces
in one explosive lightening jolt
it will kill me

i don't know if i am strong enough to die again
are you coming out you ask
i'm here and i'm terrified
i'm comfortable terrifying others
a professional don't you know
you feel me way too damn much
you say you don't like blood
but i swear you're out to get mine
there is no where to fucking hide
i didn't even know i was hiding
have i still been heart broken all this time
so we're either heart broken or in love
is there no middle ground
you are until you are not

ok i will come over this weekend and let you take care of me
you said i took such good care of you first so it's your turn
i hope i am strong enough to let myself out
and let you see me
tell you my secrets

i want to come out… all the way out
will you show me the way
it is not necessarily going to be easy
and it takes time

you may to have to push yourself a little harder
a hard cock deep inside
a seed vision planted
sitting on top of you
arms and legs pulling each other into one
you say this will be our first lesson
do you even know it's called yab yum
and i've been searching for my match for ions
sink your lips into my soul
pussy pulse so strong
dmt orgasm from touching myself
as you touch yours
you just gave it to me
over the fucking phone
jesus who are you and what the fuck is this

you feel me too much
just like that gave me all of your energy
and my soul spiraled up out from hiding
expanding my body into infinity
i promise we will do good things with this
yeah we will do good things

fuck i'm so fucked
you feel me way too fucking much
and i love it
thank you

open

girl open to him
you've opened to her
you've been moved in all directions
you are her and she needs him
yes go for it
open to him
he is different
you are different
i know you feel it
open to him because he makes you feel more of you
and that's what we are up to
this is your healing now
keep opening
open to him
he is you too

make space

make space
let the tightened chains around your hips release
unlock the chastity belt to your pleasure
it is right here i promise
breath rest lay it all down
really actually lay it down on the earth
well what are you waiting for
get horizontal on that bitch
nothing else is going to save you
you've tried it all already haven't you
so lay down and don't let a shiny false god of a man
distract you this time. although we will have wonderful stories
for lifetimes from that one

lay it down get your tired body on the ground

follow your breath

down down down

keep dropping deeper wider

empty out let go all the way exhale

this one, that one, yes him too

let go of them all so they can become compost for your new body

make space for the greatest love story you have ever known

it is already made

it is already here

do you feel it

make space

make space for some good things to happen this time

do you believe in yourself now

look at the all the shit you created

again and again and again

seriously grammy award winning shit bravo

and there's more bitch

so much more can you feel it

can you drop into her so deeply

she begins to pick you up

you are floating flying high on the ground

all because you stopped dropped and rolled

get down there and stay down there until she decides

when to stand up you will feel it

there will be no doubt no question no confusion

make space

this spaciousness will feel like liberation and home at the same time

yes there you are again

i love you

i love when you come so close

thank you for making space

for what matters

making space matter

so make space for great matter

your voice

i wish you were coming over
so i could make coffee in the morning for you
i want to see the shapes your words make
as they come out of your mouth
do they match the sing song sound
of your voice that i love so much
always sounds like smiling
even when you're sad or mad
you are mad
please don't stop talking
i want to write my stories in the morning
as we sip coffee and you build us a fire
and find your new car love of the moment
i wish you were coming over
i'm sorry i moved so far away
let's change that
i get lost in your words
we've been on the phone for hours
i spin in circles trying to keep up
or down i've lost track of the ground
i have no idea what you are saying
i love your voice
please don't stop talking

Sally Stower

Sally lives & writes from a remote fishing shack
on the southern coast of Australia.
She navigates her life by writing & storytelling
and riding the wild weather & seas.

She runs a full-time private practice online
as a somatic trauma therapist, coach & speaker.
Her shack life provides the perfect backdrop
to write & experience life fully in the elements,
helping and assisting people from all walks of life all over the world,
to find their way back home to themselves,
to others & to their environment.

Storytelling, myths, reading books & music
are what she loves to deep dive into
in her spare time under a kerosene lamp and candles
with her furs at night by the sea.

The Fox & Me

Where are you fox? Are you there? Come to me. I am here. Stop stalking me. I am ready. Come on! Show yourself!

Hunting
Pursuing
Summoning
Tracking
Stalking

This divine young man enters my world obsessed with fox furs. He adores the fox. He worships the furs, unrelenting, in his every thought. He wakes in the middle of the night, his hardworking hands feel the soft and sensual items. I salivate at the thought of watching him with the furs, how he moves, how he engages with the fox. Deeply immersed, I'm seduced and taken to another world. His obsession has become my edge. He urges me to buy fox furs, to wear them, to hold them, to be with them.

I hang out in the uncertainty and dance with him on the edges. Back and forth, he comes close then backs off into the forest. Is he timid and shy? Or are his steps stealth like and cunning? He hunts me. He tracks me down through the forest. I can't help but be mesmerized by his intensity and his focus with his divine furs. I can't sleep at night. I've now become nocturnal.

Is he the fox? Or is he the fox hunter?! And I am the fox!! Does he lust for me? Is he drawn to my scent? Is he wanting to hunt me? To capture, to devour me? To rub his face in my fur? To lose himself in me?!

Who is this divine fox man?
Is this fox hunter, a messenger?
Guiding me to the fox medicine?
Inviting me to journey with the fox?

To discover the fox in me? Who is that woman?
That fox woman? That fox woman in me.

Red fox head pelt wrapped around my shoulders. Am I a shaman!
Beating her drum, calling in the spirits. Traveling to the underworld,
walking the path to the 'other side' and bringing back lost parts. A
'calling' to bridge two worlds to dance on the edge of both realities.
Delicate fox fur stole wrapped around my shoulders. Am I a fox
woman, a sensual desirable lure for all men?! Is he waking up the
fox in me? As I howl in the dark night naked. Feeling into my fur,
evoking the essence inside me, moving with the dance of my fur.
Sensual, alluring demanding. Spewing off the scent of a woman that
no man can resist. How she walks how she talks. The fox inside me.
Born to wear her fur, born to have fox skin!

Is this fox medicine inside me? Is this fox guiding me through life,
navigating me through dark forests, the consecutive dark nights of
the soul? Journeying through enchanted forest adventures. Sniffing
out danger. Showing me the path with her fox footprints. Teaching
me to trust my instincts, follow my impulses, overcome adversity,
adapt to change, guide me on transformative journeys. Is this fox
ensuring I live a full, rich & deep life?

Who is this desirable fox?
Ducking Weaving
Stealth like Shapeshifting
Appearing then disappearing

Who is this delicious alluring enticing man? Is he a fox, or is he the
fox hunter? Who is this fox? Is it me? The fox woman. The fox
medicine in me? I'm in the dark, blindfolded. I'm brought to my
knees in anticipation, bathing in curiosity, dripping with anticipation.
The not knowing is killing me, I am dying to know!

Where is the fox hunter? The lover of fox fur
The pursuer of my scent

Finally he vanishes. Gone. Poof! Just like that. Retreated into the woods. Disappeared. No warning sign, nothing but a deathly and deafening silence. Is this wild fox woman too much? Has he discovered a more delicious scent?

Did this even happen? Have I been caught in a myth? Am I somewhere between two worlds? Is the medicine being born and the truth unfolding as we speak. Has he been sent for me to journey with the fox medicine, the fox myth. Has he just passed me the medicine bag. Was he sent as a message, to nudge me, to guide me to the lost parts of me. To discover my inner world at depths I'd never imagine. Was he sent into my physical realm to find the fox in me? Reignite what is already alive in me? To tantalize me, to seduce me, to surprise me, to bring me back to life? Did the myth send me this fox hunter to me..

TO DISCOVER MY OWN SCENT?!

Woman without a Tongue but with her Skin
[Unedited, uncut, raw]
Melbourne, Victoria, Australia most locked down city in the world
[2020-2022] Premier Dan Andrews

Stop, wait
Shock
What the fuck?!
Danger
Anger, fighting
Deception, confusion
People divided, families destroyed
Silenced, masked

Entrapped
World gone mad
Quick!! move!!
Fuck!! Trapped! Locked down!! Again!!
Two whole fucking years!!
Over and over
Lock down after lockdown
Dan's "Ring of Steel" held firm
Brutal Martial law
Most locked down city in the world

Trapped in my tiny inner city apartment
Thirty eight square meters, windows of walls
City of darkness
Aloud out only 1 fuck'n hour a day
No visitors allowed
Neighbors turned against each other
Faceless angry people
Nowhere to go, nowhere to hide
Ostracized laughed at, abused, ridiculed, rejected, exiled
Why.. because I decided to take a different path?!
I can't get out
Relentless, forever
Never to see the light again
Trapped in the prison of my own home
Walls caving in
Isolated
Going mad
Giving up
Scrolling social media trapped within four walls
Everyone interstate & overseas going about their normal business
Photos at the beaches, restaurant food pics. What the fuck?!
No one coming to get me out
I'm crying for help but no one can hear me
All alone, going mad!!

No pets, no plants, no other humans
Just me, alone, isolated
Tending to my fireplace
The only life force keeping me going
Smoldering embers
A flicker of hope

Then there was "Jerry" [the field mouse]
His grand entrance every night at dusk
Always looking up at me perplexed
Then scurry away as darkness fell
My only friend, the only unmasked face I ever saw
I welcomed his whiskers, his attitude
I longed to see him each day

I dug deep each day
I bathed with the kelp
I tended to her for 7 days and 7nights
Coarse salt strewn across the entrance
Standing strong at the doorway
I embodied Selkie everyday, without fail
Like the green statue on the rocks of the Faroe islands
Long formidable stare out my kitchen window
Standing tall, standing strong
In my hand, I held my seal skin tight

I decided to join the forces
I hit the streets. Pots and pans banging loudly
I fought the good fight
Then turned inwards
Packed my bags
Time to run. Get out!
Dust swept up by the Wicked Warlock North's broom
Fuck you Dan Andrews!! Dictator Dan!
You criminal, You tyrant! You inhumane man!!

You should be locked up forever! The key thrown away!
I despise you!!
Escape, chaos, upheaval
Six lockdowns already, surely not again!
Dorothy no shoes
Quick grab your skin. Barefoot. Quick move fast
In the dead of the night
A Jeep, a bag & my skin

Lost days, lost time
Disorientated, depleted
No energy, no soul
Two whole fucking years of being isolated
No touch, no hugs, no people's faces
Starved of connection
Starved of touch
Starved of a humane life
Suffocated in ISOLATION. All alone
My body in collapse
Lost all hope. Lost all will to live

Depleted. Soul wounded. Sharp rocks
Feet crying out loud in pain
"You can't do this!"
"Keep going, you can!"
"Don't think, just do!"

Blindfolded, I can't see
None of this makes sense. Follow your instinct
"But I don't know where I'm going?"
Sniff the road
Fear unfolding
Pain, hurt, doubt. Close your eyes
Don't listen to the noise, to the judgments, to the naysayers

Cross the border, get out!!
Follow the scent
Don't give up. Keep going don't stop
Are you crazy? What the fuck?
Is this actually possible?
Thud! Land! Boom!!
I did it

Stop, Quiet
Body settling, mind adjusting
Soul landing. Orienting, arriving
I made it. I'm here
Stop, Heal
Gather your thoughts. Mend your soul
Quieten your tongue
There are no words
Relax into your seat
Watch the waves roll in. Hear the thunder
Hear your heart beat. Taste the salt on your lips
Immerse in nature
You are now safe. You are now free
You have arrived. Its over

Stop, you made it
Give space now
Heal, build your strength
Reflect, take your time
There is no rush now
Take it in, you did it!
You escaped!!
Your "Fisherwomen's Shack"
Your remote home by the sea
Selkie is finally home
She made it
"I did it!"

Reclaiming My Southern Cross

Its 4am in the morning & I step out onto the deck
Pitch black & the night is a deep dark
I gaze out across the ocean
The brisk Antarctic air bracing my body
Waking my face abruptly
My body quivers

Hovering right on the horizon, directly in front of me
Like a slap in the face
The "Southern Cross" turned upside down
The Crucifix in perfect formation, but on its head
Staked in the ground, on the horizon out at sea
The only constellation in clear view
The rest of the night sky a blanket of clouds
A statement, clear for me to see
The brightness of each star blinding
A blunt sign that can't be ignored

Hung like the tarot "Hanged Man"
Unusual, haunting, captivating
It spooked me, sent shivers through my body
Unnerving Unsettling
I stood frozen
I've known her all my life
Never have I seen her this way!
Is that possible? Am I really seeing this?
As if the whole night sky tipped sideways
The Milky Way surrendering
Its sword laid down

Boom, like a bolt of lightening
There is no doubt
The shocking betrayal

A deceitful ending
A distant but haunting memory

You no longer have a hold on me
You are hung upside down by your feet
The Pointers still point to the South
The direction more clear than it's ever been
NOT to your homeland
But to MY STORY, not yours!
I reclaim the Stars!
I reclaim the Southern Cross!
I reclaim the South!
I reclaim the Direction!
I face South, now standing strong!

Reclaiming my body
Reclaiming myself
Reclaiming my direction
Reclaiming my ground, my feet

I stand strong on the deck of MY remote fisherwoman shack
Selkie, the seal woman statue on the rocks of Faroe Islands
Holding my skin in my hand
My seal woman's strength infused in my bones
Etched deep within my soul

An ending of you and the hold you have had on me all these years
He who betrayed me, I release you!!
No more!
The end.
Back to me.

Wounded Selkie - the sisterhood

The belting winds of winter are on their way
The storms are coming
Anticipation building. Pressure building
Feeling the tension
Deadline looming
I have to leave the craggy shore
And dive back into the sea
Before it's too late!

Standing on the edge of the precipice of something deep
no rope, no harness, nothing to hold

The rugged coastline, the wild shores
I must join the women
Because that's what the selfie story says right?
In the distance
In the bowels of the deep ocean
I can not see them
But I know they are there

I'm standing on the shore
Feeling naked, bare, exposed
Decades to find my skin
She is with me. I wear her, all of her
But I can not take the plunge
It's dark, The sky is black. Not a star to be found
No way to navigate
The waves crashing on the shore
The storm is brewing. The anticipation building
It's cold. My teeth are chattering
My seal fur turning inwards
I'm standing on my flipper toes
Looking out to sea

I hear one voice
"Come join us!"
But then I lower my head in shame and despair.
I can not! I must! I can not! I must!
How to do?
Stuck
Frozen
Moving awkwardly, shyly
From left to right
Feeling swallowed up by the fear
The wounded seal
It's too dangerous to join them
I've been there before
Broken. Betrayed. Hurt. Deep wounds.

Sisterhood what is that?! Nothing but pain
Stabbed deep through my severed heart
I've bled for a lifetime
Perhaps even generations
With tears of betrayal by women
And I know the selkie myth tells me I must join them
But I don't know how
I've only ever swam alone
The ocean my home
Being held in her womb
Gliding through the waters
I'm free when I swim alone
I am safe when I'm alone
My seal feet are blistered from trekking for miles
over sharp broken rocks to get here.
And now I can not take the final step

I feel the call. The wind is coming
Storms are coming. The rain is coming. I must go. To join them
But I don't now how

Deep into an Endless Hole - Let the Myth Hold You!

Falling into the deep abyss. I can't feel my feet
Falling Falling
No one coming
My hand empty
My feet crumbling
My heart rotting
There is no ground
Silent dark nothingness
Deep into an endless hole

Trust in the story. Trust in its unfolding
There is someone guiding you
It's all a mystery. But you are HELD in the mystery
Trust in the divine spirit. Trust in the mystery
You are not alone! That is an old story! Let it go, set it free!

You have strength in your heart now
You have strength in your legs
In your hips, in your thighs
Your womb is solid
Stand tall on the rock
Hold your skin confidently
You have yourself
You have you!
The ocean is your home
The rock face your ground
The forest your discovery & your refuge
Your curves
Your beauty
You are formidable
You don't need anyone else
You are enough!
The story, the myth unfolding

Open the bag of medicine, look deep into its pockets
The answers will come. In time you will realize
Take the medicine
Turn the bag upside down
Lean into it, fall into it, hold it, digest it
Even just notice it
Accept the medicine, trust the medicine
You are being guided
The mystery divine
Everything is as it needs to be

Let your breath settle
Let your feet touch the ground
Soften your gaze
Allow your muscles to melt
Yield into my lap and into my heart
You are safe
You are held
I'm here
It is OK
We will be OK
Together
You and me
The Myth & me!

Battle down the Hatches – Full Moon [Dark Winter Night]

Its 2am. Am sitting in the dark in my remote seaside humble fisherwoman's shack. The winds are wild and the ocean is swelling, bursting at the seams. There's no weather stations out here so don't really know how strong the gales are or high the ocean tide is or will be. How far will it go? Its pitch black. Blistering antarctic winds thrash my shack back & forth. The "south westerlies" wild & formidable. Exposed to the elements. WILD, UNTAMED, RUGGED. Harsh & certainly not for the feint hearted! I can't sleep.

The anticipation building & building as the wind is pounding & thrashing, howling through the gaps in my window sills. Rain bubbling up from the window tracks. The windows banging & shaking. The doors knocking, the tin roof battered by her wrath. How far will she go? How will my shack hold up?

I sit braced in the dark—Drambuie in hand. Candle burning. Flickering, dancing. All rugged up. Heated blanket. The warmth on my legs calming my nervous system. Wrapped in mothers arms. Sheltered from the storm

The wind. She is dynamic & powerful beyond imagination. She has no reigns. She travels solo. She needs no other. She takes no prisoners. She has no conscience. She is determined. She knows her own roar. She makes no excuses. She is unapologetic. She doesn't hold back. She beats to her own drum. Drives forth on her own path. Carves, slices, dices. Whips up her beauty! Makes us pay attention to her. Unapologetically herself. She engulfs us all.

There is no monitor for her. No way to track her power. No weather station here along the coast. So eerie, but I'm excited and exhilarated. It's just me and her. Wild & remote. In the elements, free!

I peek out my kitchen window. In the feint light I can see the shoreline. The ocean retreated to low tide. Yet to feel her full force. My wildness evoked at the thought of her full tide tomorrow. In the eye of the storm. How will they interact…wind & ocean? Together in force or fight in battle. Will the wind whip her up into a fury? Or will the sea fight back and in the midst of this battle, will the waves thrash against my shack or just pound the rocks at my feet? Will I be carnage on the field or bear witness to these two powerful forces on the edge. Full and wild. Forever together. Wild and untamed. They wake me from a long dormant sleep. Bringing me back to life, I take my first breath I gasp for my first taste of life again. My body jolted back to existence. Back to life. On the edge

Eros Dances at Full Tide

How far can I go! I feel so alive! It's nearly FULL TIDE on a winter's FULL MOON.

I step outside of my shack into the midst of ferocious seas and storms. The wild winds thrash my body. My face wet with excitement. My feet can hardly keep their footing. The waves crash on the rocks, metres away, the tide builds & builds. I'm on the edge with anticipation. Freezing icy cold winds cut right through to my bones. Invigorated! Alive! I laugh out loud. I scream to the gods, "Thank you wind! Thank you for making me feel alive again! For waking me up from a long sleep! From my dying body & soul after years of lockdowns. I can finally taste life again!"

Are you not afraid? Are you not alone & scared? They say!

"NO! Fuck no!!!I haven't felt this alive in decades!"
MY ARMS EMBRACE THE WIND LIKE A LONG LOST
FRIEND!!

My selkie skin wants to dive into the ocean
Dance in her waters
Laugh out loud till her seal belly hurts
Flick the wind
And surf with her tail
Dunk her head in the salty waters
Taste the foam & bubbles on her tongue

The winds now getting close to 90km per hour, the swell to 7 metres.
I retreat back inside "Selkies Den". The windows shaking. The
chimney howling. The fire roaring. My fingers frozen in time. I wrap
myself up in a woolen blanket & furs, get warm by the fire, crack
open a bottle of champagne and toast to the gods! Lift my glass to
the force of mother nature –she who is boss, and celebrate life again.
Thank you thank you!! Tears of relief fall into my champagne. Why..
because..

I FOLLOWED THE SCENT
Blindfolded on my knees
I crawled across the border
Selkie guided me here
Fox navigated me through the dark forest
So I could see again
So I could feel again
So I could feel alive again!!

"So here's to Selkie & the Fox!" I cheered and smiled. I celebrate the
Selkie in me. I celebrate the Fox in me. Thank you to the myths that
worked me, that wove their magic in me, to guide me here. I have a

front row cinema seat to the best movie of my life, unfolding in front of me!

It's almost full tide and "Selkie's Den" is riding out the storm, I am protected by her thick skin and her sturdy limestone double brick walls. She is strong. She can withstand. She is proving her thick skin. The winds so wild. My body so full of excitement. I can't sit still. I can't settle. I throw off the blanket and furs. Dorothy has definitely lost her shoes. I feel satiated & tantalized by it all. Of mother nature showing who's boss. I'm looking outwards on my tippy toes. My face pressed up against the kitchen window, on the edge. I want to join with her, meet her on the edge AGAIN.

I've never felt more alive. I can't get enough of her. I want to rip my clothes off and be with her, dance with her. The excitement alive in every cell of my body again. I want to stand on the rocks naked. Dance in the foamy waves as they crash on the me. I want to step on her toes, feel her wrath, her joy, her life force. Wind my friend, you have shown me a new beginning. Let me ride on your coat tails. Let me be guided by you.

As the tide rises to its peak
The ocean is about to scream
In her orgasm
Like a crescendo
A climax
Lust in her waves
Hot under her breadth
Pushing forth on the shores
About to blow her load

[God I'm getting dirty now. Eros aroused in me. I have no control. I surrender to her]

Don't hold me back. Argh!

I want this. I've longed for this feeling.
It's back, finally!!
An hour till she peaks
Full tide still yet to cum!
I'm not sure I can hold it in any longer.
I'm bursting in my loins.
Does it get more powerful than this?
How does she do it?! Gasp.
I scream out loud
Like in the dead of night . I roar!
And I'm doing it alone.
Arch my back
Roar till I cum! In rhythm with her
Ride her crest
Follow her lead
Let her take me there
Yes. All the way
I can taste it. Her building and building
The waves getting wilder
The wind roaring louder
The fire burning intently
Everyone in unison
Every life force uniting
Fire! Air! Water!
All alive in this moment
On the brink. On the edge
I say fuck it. I don't care!

I take off to the rocks again. I stand on the precipice of her beauty &
awe & rage! The salt air splashing my body. I'm about to take my
clothes off.. And..

Knock knock at the door. FUCK!

Eulogy

For all the beliefs that have haunted me for decades.
For a life time.
I SAY GOODBYE to…

"I'm not good enough!" I love you & I set you free
"I'm not worthy" I love you & I set you free
"I'm not wanted" I love you & I set you free
"I'm not lovable" I love you & I set you free
"I'm stupid, not intelligent" I love you & I set you free

We have been entwined forever
We have walked this path side by side
You have held my hand. Doing your best to protect me
I see you, I appreciate you
I lean into you & embrace you
But it's time to set you free

To let the Gods' hands come & hold your hand now
To take you home to the lost souls, to the other lost parts
To find your family, to let you rest
For you have worked hard, ferociously
Determined in the face of adversity
All to keep me safe!

For me to believe in all these things, has meant
that I have had to dig deep within me..
To find her, to love her, to want her
To appreciate her, to discover her gifts
To honour her wit, to celebrate her strategy
To respect her in every way

For those wounded parts have taught me to adapt,
to shapeshift, to have empathy for others.

But now I lay you to rest.
I now adapt & shapeshift according to me on MY TERMS,
to choose WHO, WHAT, WHEN & HOW,
to navigate this world, to bring forth parts of me,
to LIVE FULLY, to live my full life.
ALL PARTS OF ME! For you have forced me to live
a RICHER, FULLER life.
You have expanded my life force,
my spirit, my soul. I thank you & I set you free!!

Tombstone reads:
"You have lived a full life"
"You've left no stone unturned"
"Wild & Untamed"
"I lived life!"

The Fox & Selkie
The Selkie in me
The Fox in me
They reside in me
They're skins wrapped around me
Forever more
They ARE both me!!

Sara Marshall

Sara Marshall lives in a rural town in Somerset,
in the south-west of the United Kingdom,
with her dog, Sid.

These are her first new writings in many years.

Loose Ends

I wanted to quilt my life onto a page for you
Beautifully padded and embroidered
But I lost the thread, I dropped all the stitches
And what runs through my fingers is a tangled skein of yarn
Knotted and uneven
Impossible to weave into the tapestry I dreamt of as a child
The one with all the loose ends tucked in and hidden
And the front knotted in tight and beautiful
Instead I am in a place of unravelling
But I am not yet unravelled
I am not yet wholly undone
There must still be time to find the golden thread of my life
And root it like a vine into the earth
Weave it around the trees
Knot it into the stars
Tie it to the moon
Find the pattern of a future not yet written
And follow it, follow it
Follow it to its end.

After Red Riding Hood

I am thinking about paths we walk. The paths we walk only to be lost and the paths we find when we need to be found. The hope paths, the desire paths, the dead-end lost-in-a-maze paths, the paths that lead to water and the paths that lead to land and the paths that led me to my hands deep in the soil, grit under my nails, dirt-lined palms. The star paths, the moon paths. The paths walked over and over and over and over and over and over again, and the paths never taken. The paths that end in chaos and confusion, a pile of steaming rocks, a stinking pelt.

I am thinking about the wolf. He's the black dog, he's the hunter before the hunter arrives, he's there before the red is blooming, he is there in the shadows, he is there under the bed. He is the dark soul of us all.

I didn't put breadcrumbs in my pocket or spin out a spool of silver thread when I walked out into the forest of my life, to lead me into the woods or bring me home again. I never thought that the wolf on the path would be me. But he is. He lies in wait, he honeys me with words, he shows me flowers and whispers of all the dreams of all the world, and then he swallows me whole. Into the darkness, into the belly of loss, into the deep messy mud-muck of my mind. This happens again, and again, and again.

There is a path I walk most mornings. A stony, rocky path through the woods. A river on my left, a swift shallow shining thing. The trees on my right, greening now, in early summer. Wildflowers scattered thick in the undergrowth – the shocking pink of campion, the yellow trill of archangel, the candyfloss of cowparsley and the bright stars of wild garlic – and all the green green cool greens. The ones that nourish and the ones that kill. The nettles, hogweed, willowherb; quiet lethal hemlock. Sometimes, when the wolf is in my mind, the hemlock hums its invitation.

I walk this path with my dog, this is our morning path. We walk on until the path moves from river stone to soft dark loam, until it brings us to the bluebell glade. To sit in a bluebell wood for me, is akin to sitting in an ancient church. The same heavy silence of god, beneath the birdsong, the chatter of squirrel, the coo and fluttering of wood pigeon. To sit in a bluebell wood, surrounded by ancient mossy trees, is to sit alongside the otherworld. It is a magical place, a place of protection. The wolf never comes here.

I've walked many paths, we all have. It's what we do, we are ever moving, ever seeking, a constant physical or mental migration that is in our blood now. We remember deep roots, living in the heart-place, drinking the cool still waters of a forever home; we remember this belonging in the very depths of our beings but it is a lost thing, a dream, a grail.

I am thinking of the steps I took that led me to where I am now. The steps I took, the skins I wore. The steps I didn't take, and the all the different skins I shed. The forks in the road, snake-tongues flickering and hissing, charming endings from music that never played, ghost echoes back through the years. Layer on memory layer, shadow on shadow, paths weaving together and apart, criss-crossing, tearing asunder. I have been chameleon, I am a shape-shifter.

I have been lover to men who loved me and men who never did and men who never could. I have been mother to children who were not mine, and I have been not-mother to my only child. So many skins I wrapped myself in only to find they did not fit at all And I still, still, still do not know which skin to call my own.

Listen with (step)mother

I made sure I got her early, when she learnt to read, in fact. I showed
her that the real world wasn't like the world of stories and that's your
fault, I said. I told the mother of her best friend that she was a selfish
little girl, and she told her oh she told her. I told her she was too
clumsy for ballet class. I told her she didn't have the right tote to
carry her ballet shoes - the little red case, with the mirror inside. You
don't dress right, I said, with your charity shop finds. Your hair is
too straight, too short, or the wrong colour. I told her no one wanted
her at parties. I told her she couldn't dance. When she wanted to go
to a school where she could learn Latin (those stories again!), I told
her she wasn't clever enough for a different life. I told her those who
had called her gifted, and taught her Anglo-Saxon poetry at 10 years
old, they were just joking, making fun of her. When she failed the
entrance exam I said, see? See, see, see? You are no good, will
never be any good. Get down. Stay down.

She would keep fighting though. Stubborn. Always so stubborn.
She found a way through with her words that carried her through the
years to university; she even dared to act. To become someone else,
every so often. Even though even then I would whisper in her ear,
you fake you fraud they see straight through you they all know you
are nothing. You are ridiculous to them. They hate you, they laugh
at you. She closed her ears and eyes to me but I waited. I bided my
time. Wicked step mothers have all the time in the world.

I waited for her to start loving and then I found the way into her
heart, through the cracks someone else put there. I didn't do that.
But he did his job well. So many cracks, so many pieces, for me to
keep from healing, to keep open, red raw and bleeding. They will all
do that to you, I said. You will never, ever be good enough. You will
never be what they want. That's why he didn't want you. You are
boring. You don't have anything interesting to say. You don't listen
to the right music, you don't know the right people, you still wear the

wrong clothes. You don't fit into this world or any world. Why why why do you keep trying? Get down. Stay down.

Still she fought me. Put her mind to work. Plays and poetry and other people's words to fill her up and crowd me out. Six long university years. And then I told her, what good are you without a First? I told her, everyone in your Masters class got a Distinction. It means nothing. You are nothing. And she, she, she finally believed me. Gave it all up, flew to the other side of the world to be free of me. But I clung to the hem of her skirt, slipped into her pocket, packed myself in her suitcase. And when she arrived - surprise! Here I am!! She wasn't that pleased to see me. Hadn't I already done enough?

Darling you're only 25 I said! There's plenty of time yet for you and me. We're in this for life don't you see? I have so much more to tell you. Are you sitting comfortably?

Then we'll begin.

To my father, after Vasilisa

Ever since you died, daddy,
I have been running from death
From endings
From collapse
Hanging onto broken glass with bleeding fingers
Clinging to crumbling walls with torn nails
Holding onto rot
Holding onto dust and ashes
Holding onto what I should not

I've slept behind walls of thorn
And watched rose petals drop
And I've let the wolves in to feast
On sorrow
And anxiety
And on my courage

Letting their dark paws trample my dreams
Only occasionally glimpsing the size of their teeth
Keeping my eyes shut
I did what I needed to do to survive, daddy
I still do it

But life life life,
Not all of it but some of it,
Not all the time but some of it,
Has been passing me by.
The deeper mysteries,
Knowledge too, and wisdom
The most brilliant of joys
The bravest of adventures
All riding by
As I wait, in the forest,

In the trees,
On the edge of the village.
Hesitating.

Too scared to return, or to act
Too afraid to listen to the doll
As she sits in my pocket
(My wild self, my soul self)
Because she would tell me
(and she tells me)
(and I hear her)
That now is the time to let go
To let what needs to die, die
To let what needs to end, end

Now it is time it is time it is time
To let the wheel spin
And step
      Into
         The
            Abyss

Do I trust the doll, daddy?
Daddy, do I trust the doll?

(I am still running)

Vision

Lady heron,
Solitary grey huntress
Trailing her skirts in the stream
Gathers her goddess gown and glides
In slow silver silence to her throne bough
There, resplendent in her mystery
She surveys her watery kingdom
Casting her gaze majestic from side to side
She looks at everything but me
And I look at nothing but her

Time stills and the air hushes
Heavy with her power
The rain weeps into the woods
And I ask her
And she speaks
She says

Wait wait be still
The power of your waiting will bring you
What is for you
in this world and in the other

See my patience as I wait for the silver fish in the clear stream
I wait, he comes
Wait wait be still
She says
But do not wait too long

There is a wasteland beyond these trees
And the wasteland is growing
Do not let it take more than you have given it
There has been sacrifice enough

And your blood will run thin and cold
You must drink the healing waters
You must heal the wounds you can

You are not alone well-maiden,
I hear your sisters weeping
But I hear them laughing too

Listen, don't you?

There is still joy in this world if you will go and find it
You will be safe in your wanderings
I grant you safe passage

She says I am not your story
This is my place and it is not yours
You cannot stay here

You are human and I am heron
And I have seen it all before
And you have not

You must go out and gather in new greening
Begin the reforestation of your soul
Work in this healing of this land
It is the work it is the only work

And time shifts and shudders
As she lifts into the air
With her heavy grey wings
Silent messenger
Cloaking herself once more
In the mist
She vanishes

Kintsugi

I see the changing I see it
I feel the shifting I feel it
The mask is slipping
The ground beneath our feet
Is opening up

We are breaking
We are shattering
We are shattered
Broken into pieces

This unchanging ever-changing world of men
Is shrugging off its skin
Empty ideas and words and thinking
Desiccating and shriveling
Accelerating to the new
Leaving its slowworm tail,
Leaving its snake trail,
In the dust

See
It
Go

Fragile facades crumbling
Spitting smoke and fire from the cracks
Darkness is seeping and bleeding into the light
And the phoenix are rising
Shaking their tail feathers
Sending the sparks of their burning
Into the cold starred sky
Stretching their wings
Into the flames of their own dying

Transforming their destruction
Into new creation
Even as creation dissolves
And reassembles
New forms firing
New ideas firing

The shattered reforming
Soldered with bright shining lines
Golden shining lines
Of truth

Prompt i

My day is spent searching for words
Elusive words
Words that don't want to be found
Or do want to be found
But won't admit it
Words that hide on the edges
In the hedgerows
In the creatures that dwell there
Words that fly with the birds overhead
Words that hide on the margins
On the liminal land
Between shore and sea
Gull, curlew, goose coming in to rest
Words that tumble with the water
From the face of mountains
That speak in secret green voices
Words that hide in fallen leaves
And whisper beneath the feet
My days are spent searching
For all the words that are spoken
That we cannot hear
My days are spent searching
For all those words
That need a voice

Prompt ii

There is an ache inside of me
That releases with the sudden sharp shock of immersion
I am reskinned, reshaped, in the deep blue
I wear the water like silk on my bones
Bubbles like jewels on my fingers and toes
I am a water animal
Limbs stretch and release,
Tumbling, turning, diving
Damselflies dance their dazzling desire dance
Trip their turquoise tango across still waters
Starfished, weightless, held
I float beneath the arcing blue
Exhaling untold stories to the quarter moon

After Amangon

Waiting, waiting, waiting in the well
To rise, to return, to rejoice with my sisters
To hold the healing waters in my hands
Bring a flooding abundance of healing
To a broken savaged land
I wait I wait I wait
Deep deep here in the well
Where I hide from the fire of men
From their stinking smoke
And their stinking fire words
If they drank from my hands now
It would be bitter water
Salted by my tears, grief, anger, rage
They would taste death not life
Take into themselves the poisons they have spread
And choke on it
There are men of this age who should never drink
At the glittering eternal well
They poison it with their lips, their lies
They seek to transform all that is good
To all that is rot and ruin
I see them I see them I see them
And
Fuck
Them
Their pride, their egos
Their bigotry, their hate
Their messiah complexes
Their misogyny
Their darkness, their ignorance
Their violence
Their never-ending ever-lasting guns
Power hungry

War obsessed
And blind to it all
Does nothing ever change?

Will nothing ever change?

Midsummer Nights' Dreams

Seeds in the dying grasses
Spill pollen drifts
When the wind blows soft
And the meadow sways.
Sky scarlet gold.
I missed the moon,
Always too early to catch the moon.
Sleeping dreaming
Those jellyfish dreams,
I see them in the mirror
When I cannot find the light.
Words words words
Stuck, stuck
Now the crow is cawing its silence
And the candle burns.
Scarlet poppies in the corn
Look to lost wings overhead
I have swum with the swans at midwinter
I remember the mist

Lament

And the rain falls and the rain falls
And I wonder
What if I never find my skin at all?
When the clouds roll in
And the waves crash on my shore
And there are no singing songs
In the deep dead dark of night
Will I be left landlocked?
If I do not find it how can I be?
If I do not find it who can I be?
I am shape without form
Dissipating desiccating ghost
Nothing fits nothing fits nothing fits
I am a lock without a key
I am an answer without a question
When my scent is lost to me
How will I know myself?
Will I sing my selkie song in silence?
Wandering in this wasteland world
Unseen unheard
A faint forgotten story
Sisters call me in!
Sing me your calling songs
In these grey days
These grave days
Sing me home

Letting go

You are enough in and of yourself
You are enough
It is time to stop
The fighting to be more
Or less
Or anything other than yourself
Because you are enough
It is time to let go of the not good enough
The should have been, the could have been
Let go let go let go
It is time to hear the words that praise you
And not damp them down in the dark
Or hide them in corners
Or only bring them out once a year
To bask in their memory
Hear those voices all the time
Let them speak to you and wash away the doubts
Believe them, let them shine
And you shine with them
You shine
You are enough in and of yourself
Have the courage to know
It is time to be enough
It is time to be enough
It is time

Prompt iii

I am retrieving myself piece by piece
Gathering up my old bones
The ones that are fragile and dry
The ones that have broken
And healed in strange and painful ways
I am gathering up my hair
And letting it down
Unbrushed, uncombed, unrestrained
I am going to grow into my white locks
And shine in the dark
Like a candle
I am sharpening my nails
To fight the wolves that will surely bang on the door
This coming winter
I am opening up my eyes
Wiping them clear of the sand of sleep
Practicing a clear gaze, a level gaze
That will see over mountains and oceans
And not be afraid
I am gathering up the pieces of my heart
Soldering them together with gold
This broken vessel, healed stronger now than ever
I am finding all the whispers of my lost voice
And raising them into a battle cry
Into a song, into an opera
I am singing it to my bones and reminding them
How to live again

Now I am a fox

Red russet roaming
Bright eyes in the gloaming
Feral, free
I am fox now
I am fox

I know now
There is no returning
To the beginning
Wearing the skin
I am in

I have been gifted the gift of me
And if you try to keep me
From the me of me
I will take your heart in my mouth
And leave you empty, soul blind,
Longing for my touch, my scent
My true self
Your other self

And I run

Unfettered in the freezing night
All that is past pushed behind
All that is ahead scribing story in the stars
As each paw drums the earth
A flame catches in the dark
Firebrand tail spins sparks to the sky
My wild and shrieking cry
Yips ecstasy to the elements
In my running
I create constellations
I grow galaxies
From my wild and lonesome dreaming

Els Liekens

Having travelled life's experiences in all possible directions,
Els now finds herself doing what she loves
by facilitating alchemical bodywork, breath work, yoga
and hosting plant ceremonies.

She loves expressing herself
by creating, painting, writing, singing, traveling,
and so much more.

She lives with
her three wonderful children
and loves to surround herself with close relatives.

Feeling the greatest gift
of all: to be nothing, and everything at once, in one.

Grandmother lineage

Shredding skins, feeling bones, boney stoney to the ground.
No flesh of protection keeping me safe out of the deepest grief
of loss and despair. Where are my feet?
Hanging upside down I cannot pulse my way through
The ground seems so far away.
As earth is to carry me, in which form will I present myself?
Overthrown with the seeds of feelings that my bones cannot contain,
the skeleton falls apart.
Left in the desert of dried tears in the fire pit of destruction
Waiting. Dying
Reversing life with death and life with breath.
A breeze of fresh air reaches me
Filled with the scent of raw blood
Draining my long hairs
Cluttering in strings
I feel deeply
Connecting the strings and repairing the bones
Collecting
Restoring
Waiting for no one to come
Anger reaches me,
Flows and burst up to my veins
Growing like rivers with terror
But alive
The fire returns
Flesh grows out of raging fire and I stand
Proud. Me
Living and dying
Throwing my divinity at the feet of the children I birthed
Flesh, flesh, blood, breath
Living amongst the death.
Dying in each moment
To live in eternity

Ilina

My heart is bleeding as I know I cannot reach her
I walk and talk and still, the fear
She is near, she is here, but as I know, not for long anymore
My heart is bleeding
Hands trying to reach, embrace, feel
Taking her scent in me,
Filling me with her energy
So I can walk on, knowing in remembering
Already so close
She sleeps as I watch her, I feel her, and still, I know
Capturing each moment, so precise
Trying to store it for the day
everything will fade away
Dearest, sweetest, lovely flower
with the spirit of freedom and life in its purest awareness
I will miss you
So please let me see you
Can I walk with you a little longer
As I know the shadow will come
when all life disappears from me
Can I sit with you a little longer
Taking in your beautiful hair and eyes, so I can let go,
For I will know
The forest is your home
I will know it is you
And I will still be here
Calling your name, dreaming of you
Until the whispers disappear
Remaining what is left of you
A memory
Energy flowing through
And I will know
It is you

199

The still centre, the silent house

Sssshhhhhh…
  Hhhhhhh……..
    Ssshhhhhhhhhh…….
      Sssshhhhhhhhhh……

Can you hear that?
  No, no, be still
    No words
      Only
        Listen
          Silence
            Silence

earsplitting, louder than any sound in the world

The silence
  Comes in
    ShOuF …. sHOUf … SHOUFFFF…..
                    SHhhhhhhhh……

filling everything, adding up, even more
    Every moment
      Yet another eternity of space
        Silentness- ness - nesssss…
Beauty, so profound,
  More, more,
    Deeper, deepest
      Sshhhhhh….
        Don't wake her up

Silence,
  Never sleeps
    Now listen

I've been a 1000 different women

I have been,
All that is
All that lives

Like a seed in the soil which will sprout
Its way out
Small and tender
Growing
Finding its way to the first sunlight to catch

Growing still,
Growing stronger
What once was green turns to wood
Hard, dark, strong
Stronger and bigger,
the stem bursts and scratches appear
Scars of life

The tree carries it all
Life expands to its roots
The branches, flowers, leaves and fruits,
The roots and the stem and all it is carrying
For animals and birds,
It covers a home there, too

So can you say
The tree is just it's stem,
it's leaves,
it's roots,
it's seeds

A thousand different things, it feeds.

Eros love

With the light-hearted as a flame
I feel a burst of pain
but it won't tackle me
again
for who am I to doubt
As the wheel of life is turning and swirling
inside of me
and nature that provides
the flowers and the bee
the sweet taste of honey
and the leaves falling from a tree
there I stand lifting my hands to thee
Great
almighty
mystery
show us your divinity
providing life force with all its might
and newborn stars shining so bright
making love with this sweet earth
connecting us to soul at birth
love songs echoing out loud
so will we dance on this holy ground
to its never ending sound
for the birds that fly
so high
in the blue eyed beloved sky
so will I
connect to inner freedom
and finally,
lastly
fly

Six Swans

Oh those silent years.
Six. Silent. Lonely. Years.
My oh my I have been sowing, sowing, seeking flowers
and no word.
No. Single. Word.
My fingers weaving and sowing
each and every thread.
Dedicated to restore. Dedicated.
Fully in surrender those lonely years.
They took my mother, my brother, and my father.
But oh, my own. Children.
Screaming inside, the silent façade covering my greatest, loudest,
indescribable screams.
Silence grows and still, I sow.
They can blame me, accuse me, sentence me to death,
bring fire to my flesh and yet I know: My heart is pure.
Oh the freedom when it's done!
Freedom, there is my voice again!
One beautiful swan wing remaining as a doorway to magic
and the purity of white.
Scars. But how I have been silently loved and taken care of by his
higher power of male compassion.
Love. Tenderness. I feel relieved, so free I can be, to say it all.
The curse is done. And so, life won.
I dedicated, I loved, in every moment of the task they put upon me.
I became. I loved, in every moment, because I remembered.
I remembered because I felt. I felt because I loved.
And they, loved me. And so I love.
This voice, this choice. To step inside.
My intuition worth wide. There is nothing other than this.
To be. Free free free.
Finally.

I have to trust what was given to me, if I'll have to trust anything

Trust, my dear, trust, through the dust
There will be knowing, in trust
Trust, you must, trust
Shush, hush hush
Breathe it slowly
On repeat
What was given—all this life
What was taken—so many things
But sadness, and grief only emerge
If you have loved
So deeply
So trust, my child
Trust
Love does not flee
Nor will it stay
It just is
Always and never ending
Trust your knowing
The holiness of life is ever protective
Seductive, contagious and brave
You must stand
Take this dance
In full surrender
Let go, let go
Trust and you will know
What is always will, the love of never ending fairy tale
Trust, child, trust
It was never taken away
What was given
To your soul
Always belongs
As you are whole

The Skull Tale of Fire

I am the skull
The face of death
With light
      Inside
Fire, fire to light the way,
To guide you home through the darkest night
I am the skull that has only to see, to be
The skull
That part of story when returning home begins
When light shines poorly but just enough to see
Step by step
Returning home
Trusting
Trusting the night, the inner knowing and guidance of
something beyond humankind.
Guiding, home
Home
      HOME!
Home is my place
To where… I don't know; but for now I will trust
And follow the light through the dark
The spoken voice comes from a far away place
Long ago
Lifetimes, cycles in time returning to this wisdom of speech and
guidance
Guidance
Trust
Intuition
Knowledge
Fire
Light
Darkness
Death

Cycles of life
I will return home.
To be, where I shall be guided
Do not worry and do not hurry
All is well
Returning home
To your own self

Selkie Story -The One with the Watery Mother

I am the one with the watery mother.
The mother who died a thousand times
For me to survive
Mother mother of the water
You left and you died
You left off your skin
Your family
Your everything
You gave it your life
The dance and the swirls
You slept in the dark
Alone with no self
Your skin left untouched
Abandoned
With nothing to come,
Nowhere to run
Alone in the dark
you wept all your tears

The salty taste of the sea on your lips
The smell of the ocean air
in the waves
A far remembrance of life as it was
At your place you wept and wept until tears went dry
No one to talk to, no one passed by
And there it happened, a child you brought forth
A burden to hold as you were not home
The call of the sirens
Went deep in your spine
Your soul craved and howled into the divine
The skin you were wearing a long time ago
To be found and returned
Back into your soul
As there you would stand
Dearest mother of all
The one thing your child
Would wanted for you
Go home
Return into source
To the deepest of seas
The dance of the spiral is where we grow seeds
The child kissed goodbye
And kept it in mind
The beauty of skin
And water soaked in
Mother dear mother
Thank you for life
Who knows when we meet
Until then I sing
The most beautiful tunes
Of a mother
In a soft
Selkie
skin

Water Dance

As a droplet of the sea
We dance until we set free
Where soul meets our body
We can be
As we hear the song of the siren

Automatic writing

What if I told you clothes wear mattresses
Omg green trees to sky sun upon moon
The air and groom. I love to be as shadows disappear
but what strawberry
And glow in the dark let go and see
And you know children sound so cute and holy
And fighting lover where are you
I can see a flower rose pink yellow green
As the tree tea I wish smoke hot air balloon
Let go go go of all. You are more
And family oh ice cream …yes
And making love I wish a man will come
And find me to eternity in flesh and blood
As wine in a cup movie singing drinking medicine
Is calling. Higher above the rocks and mountains and lakes I want to
swim. But falling stars and holy spirit feel the free you are no
nothing. Seeing breeding you have been
Left apart so many parts and things
Closet broken glass mirror women being whole
Belly stories. Writing this pen and feeling blessed
Just love by yourself doing this all. the sky and earth are always
sleeping there. and feel green again. we are
it's over

A Water Droplet's Life

The words will come
Cause I am at shore
I am at the shore, the sea, the ocean
The waves, waiting for the wind to carry me along,
This long distance to the earth, where I lay myself to peace
Feel the magic of the mother
Being born again
Into the earth I go and I flow
Towards a new source of inspiration and magic.
High up in the mountains, the cloud that carried me
Releases, releases all the tension and finally
Aaahhhhhh
Sets itself free
from the weight it carries over the fields and the valleys, the dark
lands and the forest, up and up and up and more, to shore
Being spiraled to the very source
of essence and renewal
Rebirth
Rebirth
Re-birth
All over again I glow, refreshed, I know
The river starts to flow
As I sprout out,
The way is beautifully carved into earth's mouth
as I flow amongst my dearest fellow drops
Flow as we go, down, down, slow
Into ponds and lakes, we flow and grow
Silent and loud, and always together
Until we splash
Oh the magic of the colours we create
We splash into a 1000 pieces in the downfall of fate
Creating beauty for everyone to see,
Waterfalls as a magical slide, so free

Wasteland ~the swamp into the pond ~the womb

The swamp
The swamp comes up
It bubbles big bells of damp and heat
And we have to take care
Of our feet
We get burned and soaked in
Never to reach out again
The swamp, the swamp
It's haunting me
Like the mangrove at the side growing its vines around my soul
Trapped in the dust of dark and mud
Oh help me release,
Let go, get out of this hole
But no. No one to hear, alone here I am
Sinking and clinging myself to some ghosts
I sink, sink, sink
Deeper within
Where it's black, and it stinks
I can not get out
To move is to die
So I will not speak for I am alone
Silent, dark, wet, the swamp
It haunted my soul,
Still trapped in this hole
Sit. Still.
     You. Will. Die.
     Oh no, again, you cry?
     There is no one my dear, so don't even try
The swamp whispered nearby
     Oh silly one, what did you think?
     You would be loved you say?
     Well that is not life
     To live is to die

That's all that we know
So sink, baby, sink
In mud and despair
The swamp, the swamp
The swamp calls me, blub, blub..
Into the womb, wobbling dobbling waving craving
The womb, the womb
The pond where it all began
Such a cozy, warm, soft, carrying place I feel
I float, I sink, I breathe under and in
I taste, the watery flowing soft glory feeling of being held
Totally
Refresh myself, wash it off
Wash – all – of – it – off
Step in
Take a leap
Dive, splash feel, play, like a dolphin, a whale, a sea horse! It's real!
Dive my darling and feel
You truly are – reborn
Heads in , totally
Full body surrounded, can you just be?
Weightless – weightless and still, here. Yes, I am – here
This is the water you were born in, do you remember me?
Just like the earth, I am here, all the time
Waiting for you, to be ready
You can breathe, can you hear the silence?
Soft blowing air into the ripples that carry away with the light of
dusk remaining off shore
Ripple ripple dripple dipple
You have been water
fire, air, and earth
We are all here
it whispers near
Remember me through time
Cleanse, child, cleanse

Cleanse and rinse,
The trauma, the death parts inside of you
Cleanse your body and spirit,
So you can be – free
From all of suffering, all destruction, all regret and sorrow
you hold
Cleanse, child, as you did before
Be water, float and sink
In full of trust
I AM the womb, you are my child
Cleanse, rinse, cry, play
Like a dolphin, you will stay
I AM your mother, you are my child,
Now live your life, be free and wild

Becoming Fox

I was the ogre in former times
Grabbing in ugliness and greedy for human food
What to be, as the ogre fades away
What a waste, what a disaster I brought forth
Transmutation
To be born again being fed up with the one eyed sight
This. Is. Not. It.
So I became the fox

The fox with its red rusty fur
Ready to take off and longing so badly to belong
To the old
To the known
To the loved ones from before
I would bang my head and lose all the drops of blood
if only I could come inside
I keep banging on that literally bloody -of my own blood- door
Open, please, please please, open up!
I've changed
I am here now, I am me now,
Making other choices
Can you please see me?
Let me in?
Bang, bang, BANG, BANG again!
Until forever, yet I'll be threatened to death
And even, then, my stubbornness for his love will keep me going
on the icy snow, till I fall.
Down. Deep. Dead.
And stars will start to appear.
Stars of another world
Am I dead yet?
Where is the happily ever after here?
This story makes me sad
Takes away all hope
As there is nothing to run to, nothing to fall back to,
But the icy snow under a new born sky
Yet alone
With blood stains on my new rusty fur
I will stay, I will remember
I am, I was, I stay, I run
The happily ever after in a dream to chase
The shaman woman can be born
And die in bloody rusty fur

213

The Heart Knows the Way

The heart knows its way home
Where am I
Lost in the desert of my body and the chaotic jungle of my mind
Trying to find the pieces of myself
But blind by the convictions and beliefs
Of nothing to find, to hide, seeking, searching,
And then it appears
A flash of sunlight catches my eye
And there I lie
I find myself naked under the blue sky
Hot rays of sun reaching my body
The mind shuts down
I can feel the warmth, the passion, the love glows from my toes
Up to my legs, hips and pelvis
Into the belly
Warm and softly
It reaches my fingers, arms and shoulders
As I find myself bathing in this beloved nature
My head glows, my crown reaches high above
as my roots grow deep in the earth
And then it blooms
The heart opens
It opens to all that I was seeking
My home in myself
Connection with all
My heart knows
It knows and shows
There's nowhere to go
For every step I take
Every where I go
I am
Home to me

She Chooses

this is not the ending...it is the beginning, of a new tale
a new way, a new day
as the fox lies in despair,
paws cracking into the old hard snow
surrounded by misty layers of air
while summer already awaits
the cold of snow and ice still shimmering in her body
the fox lies
dies
a hundred times
giving in
surrendering
until finally, and suddenly
a crack, an opening!
deep inside the body, mind, energy field of all surroundings
the crack grows wider, faster, brighter
light comes in
and fills up everything
the sun, the long awaited sun
it fills her heart with glory, passion
life itself in all expression
and then it happens
the fox returns
stands up and runs
fills its rusty fur
with all the light returning to her
showing its face towards the sky
a glimpse of a tear shining out of her eye
whispering
thank you
thank you
thank you
and so the new story emerges

the fox remembers in its unconscious times
she chose against her heart
she was captured, imprisoned, threatened to death
unrecognized by her beloved
the grief and pain she suffered
sadness, emptiness
feeling totally abandoned
lost alone without a home
she re-writes, re-rites, re-rights,
HER story
she breathes it in,
deep and full of sighs into every cell within
feels it deep into her bones
captures it as fossils carved in stones
the door of the house
is closed
closed
and closed
returning to her steps of a long forgotten past
there was her home at last
but for this time she will not bang the door
nor will blood drops fall at the snowy floor
she gracefully thanks
everything that once was
with all the love in greatest magnitude
she looks and feels the gratitude,
she will not go back to the village or to the people
to be rejected, haunted, by their weapons
for now, she chooses and decides
to fill herself with starry lights
her own pace, her own grace
her path, following her heart,
finding its way, night and day
to her own and precious
home, again

Taliesin

I am the chase, the haze, the blaze
Catching or not catching
Flying falling swimming crawling
Chase chase run dive jump and strive
To catch
       Or to escape?
Who is chasing who and what
Chasing, faster, harder, more and more
Dynamics floating around one another
Yet another constellation in the sky is born
Stars appearing in the night
Of the great hunt
Taking place in the misty chaos of multiplicity
Of life
The Goddess of it all
All - of - it.
Hunting, grunting, panting, grasping
      CATCH
         SNAP
To be born again

Stasha Ginsburg

The Wild Matryoshka.
Facilitator of (w)rites of passage.
Midwife and curator of this collection. Poet.
Life story coach. Mother. Song leader. Tarot reader.
Teacher. Nourishing soup cook.

Infinitely more whole
because of the women writers in this collection.

After the Belly

Red was in the belly. I don't know how long she was in there, but she was. Swirling in a cocktail of stories, in a stew of gloop, in a mess of chaos. Spinning in the swell with her: bones. scat. a matryoshka doll. spiderwebs. acorns. scissors. bits of fur of a fox and feathers. from a blue jay. deer antler. a catholic school uniform. a story of a long ago break from the reality of 'this is how it is'. pixie dust. shells. fire. a star. a seed. burdock burrs. poppy skeletons. two scythes, shaped like a balsamic moon. a penis. a portal. a spiral. scribbles. comfrey leaves.

After the solar flares last week, I seem to have gotten 'short circuited' by flares, by an aurora borealis reaching down to the south, to Arizona, to the red rocks. I felt as though I was plugged into a socket for a night. It reawakened long ago memories -twenty year old memories, still spinning in that wolf belly. I thought I'd gotten her out then. I did. But something awakened some slight pieces of her red cape. Something forgotten. Something needed. Something lost. Something found.

I worked with clay. I molded shapes. A wolf face. hiding behind its head, a devilish grin. Ears twisting into horns. out with the archetypes. Out with the old. Mold the old into new shapes. Mold the old shapes out of me.

I drew it. I drew the belly of the wolf and I drew what happened when Red cut open the belly, from the inside. When she emerged. She looked as though she'd been in 13th century France. Somewhat Joan of Arc-ish. Warrior like. Half furred. Tree sprouts budding out of her fur side. Carrying a basket filled with flowers, wine, bread. Forget me nots. Poppies. Bleeding hearts.

Before the belly and After the belly. It's like lifetimes. And then in the belly, the in between, the time of transition, the time of change.

The time between times. The liminal beast between stories. The place to go when transformation slinks past, pointing its finger at you, saying, "Your Turn. *Tocca Te*. It's up to you." Change, girl, change.

And so, I quit coffee. I stopped drinking the small glass of wine. No more sugar. Three weeks of purifying diet leading to this strange in between stories moment in which the solar flares quickened me, activated something, opened an old story, reminded me of an old door, and said —go, quick -get what you need and leave!

And I did. I danced into her. I stayed awake inside of her. I kicked and screamed. I resisted. I feared. Worry and anxiety are stories that keep me caught in a ball of thread. Trust and faith unwind the ball and lead me through the woods. One step in front of the other.

Some stories eat us up. Some stories, we need to eat. Some stories check in from time to time, to show us if we've grown. We crawl in, and we get spit out. Or we cut our way through inside and out. And boom. We land. On the earth. near the munching wild bunnies and deer. Listening. Returning. Changed. Integrating wolves and the color red.

Creation Song From the belly. живот. *Zhivot*. Russian for Belly. From жить, *Zhit'* to Live. Lifeforce. Belly. From where we come. Where Creativity stirs.

Creation. Soft warm creation. Spreading. Warming. Nourishing. Creation. Holy Creation. Life force. Quickening. And Rising but returning. Deep home deeper than sun. Deeper than origin but also small, so small. When small, Squeezed off. Fight. Homeland. She says I am power full. She says I am creation embodied. She says I know the truth about creation. She says I am always returning to deeper knowing.

Grandmother in the Belly

Fight. So tight and scared to write. Fight too tight Scared to Fight.
Tight in belly. Amnesia. Lost stories.

Find a thread and sew a line to your origin motherline.
She sews and she snips and she cuts the thread. She embroiders a
new story on an old cloth. Oak leaves. The color red. The word
strong. Beneath and below and beyond -a Valkryie. Woman Wise
Woman Bone Strong Strength Great Great Great Great Beyond Great
Grandmother. Not many words grandmother. Mysterious Wild
woman medicine woman grandmother. She who knows
Grandmother. She who carves, grandmother. She who wants me to
Listen deeper. Grandmother. Silence Grandmother. But also night.
And dawn. Dew Grandmother. Life Death Life Grandmother.

Red's Rebirth

I am the Daughter of Red. The Daughter of the Rising Sun. The
Daughter of the Red Cock Crowing, crowned with Fire. Feet bare,
bearing my heart, lifting my heart. Proud. I did it. I am out. I am out.
I am turned inside out and back again, a plum, ripe and succulent,
sweet. The pit, the seed of all plums before me in my mouth. I taste
and spit wisdom out. I grow new story trees. I replenish the earth
with my soul song. Strong and brave and powerful. You can be
strong and brave and powerful. Thanks be to the hard stories, the
whole stories, the belly beast stories that cracked me open. To be
here. Now. Right here now. Destiny Story. I choose this country. I
choose the unknown. I choose expansion. I choose strength. I choose
me. I choose powerful. I choose the path I am on and I choose the
time I spent in the belly. I choose life. I choose this story. And her
teaching. I choose the fur that courses freely wildly down my spine. I
choose the life I was given and I choose to repurpose. Recreate.
Rekindle the life of my Destiny. The life of my songline.

Lost Girl

I am green wood
White naked trees
Thimbleberry staining the lips, giving wine red sweet.
I am grandfather tree.
I am bushy girth, slant, bow to earth.
I am mossy blanket kissing feet.
I am the waves, the sound of lake that is an inland sea calming.
I am the known not known story beyond the sacred grove.

I am Sacred Grove. Enchantment.
Silver moon gossamer flight illuminating silver trees.
I am the not quite here, not quite there.
I am the portal in oak. The acorn in my pocket.
The thump thump heart beat of earth tree rhythm
Deep earth to deep root.
The root I am. Alive I am unfurling my wild song,
My wild earth body song.
The wild of my homeland breath.

9 Minutes In

I find myself staring
>at the kingdom. The hedge. The place where
>my grandfather was told by his grandfather
>that the kingdom sleeps.
>And it is quiet. And it is deep silence.
>It is a church. A sanctuary.
>A blessing. The hedges
>are singing my name.
>In the thorns —skeletons-
>of those who could not
>Wait. Did not listen. Could not truly see.

I could swear that the
>trees are bowing.
>Making an arch-leading
>me through. And blooms.
>White Pink.Five pointed Stars. Roses. Wild Roses.
>Wild Roses. They scent the air with mystery perfume.

I am and am not dreaming.
>I am the only thing
>Waking. I am awake
>for this moment.
>This moment is my
>Destiny.
>To wake the Rose of the Soul.
>To wake the Beauty sleeping
>at the Heart of the
>forest.
>The kind of waking
>that heralds the birth
>of the new order.
>That echoes

into the tribe
       into the kingdom
       that wakes all the
       sleeping parts
       that knits and spins
       and threads wakeful ness
       back into nature
       that embraces soul
       that is pure enough

To penetrate the inner
       layers. To penetrate
       the inner layers
          to penetrate
              the inner layers

I am here now
       and I hear
           the waterfall
              and the children laughing

       in the apple tree
          and the fire and the rose
          are again
             one.

Feed Me

Body talk belly talk. Stop feeding me the wrong things. Stop feeding me bad fats, bad starch, dead food. Stop force feeding me masculine rhythms and Cronos-ian time. Stop feeding me scary stories and war stories. Stop feeding me ancient forgetting.

Feed me truth. Shiny golden platter of Red Ruby Red Seeds.

Bountiful Cornucopias of Community Gathering.

The number thirteen.

Feed me the dark. The irrational. The sublime. Feed me the mother. The mother's stew. The mother's Stories. Thirteen Roses.

Feed me wishes. Wise woman wishes. Feed me ecstasy.

Stories heavy, laden with dew.

Feed me spindles and wheels moving synchronistically to an older, truer rhyme.

Eliminate reason.

I'll take sleep and dreams.

Feed me wolf milk.
Chthonic appetizers.

Mystery seeds. Syrupy, pungent, Bitter roots.

Feed me hunger.
Feed me longing.
Even pain and suffering, but the digestible kind.

In Here I am

Here I am inside of this vastness. Stomach rumbling. Ribcage tight.
Belly loose. Inside of the belly of anticipation. Of being more naked.
Of being more clown nose. It's scary in here but it isn't. It's harder
with a screen but it is also important. It is the truth of how I journey
into the land, into the landscape of self. I have resistance. I have
discomfort here. I have doubt but I also have power. Raw power.
Truth. In that is beauty. Sleeping beauty wakening. She stirs all the
day and sometimes rises.

What I really want to say is: you can't always force her to speak. You
can't force her to open her eyes. You can't force a rose to open. You
can't always get what you want. You can't always make the pot turn
the ingredients into a magical potion. With Cerridwen, it was a year
and a day. With beauty, it was 100 years. With me, it's a mystery.
She is like a violet beneath the pines. But sometime she is wild
toothed, one eyed, more real than fantasy, cackling, lifting her skirts
and dancing her baudy dance of words.

The Birdsong Wilderness

The birdsong wilderness. She knows what she knows inside the
silence. Inside the still center. Being in a state of sleep does not mean
all is unmoving. There is breath between form. Outbreath. The
journey between lives. The still death between stories. When it is
time to awaken she does in her own quiet rhythm. In her own timing
In her innermost treasured rose self at the center of self. Rose bud
hidden from thorns. When it is time to awaken, she awakens.

Trust

I have to trust what was given to me if I am to trust anything. I have to trust this doubt if I am to trust anything. I have to trust this fear if I am to trust anything. I have to trust this confusion if I am to trust anything. I have to trust what was given to me if I am to trust anything. I have to trust this stickiness. I have to trust this mystery. I have to trust this holy wild remembering. I have to trust this grief. I have to trust this anger. I have to trust this story. It is and it is not fixed. It is and it is not a sentence. It is and it is not a mystery. Known/Unknown.

Bloom

Pornographic flower opening. I can see down her silk throat —down inside where pollen flickers like a thousand soft petalled teeth. I want to put my fingers inside of her. I want to lick the sticky outer edges, take in the whole holy scent of her. Soft, so soft, emerging from hard, spiky prickles of desert cactus. Conserve water. Parch. Dry. Without rain for centuries. Stone hard, stone dry. Rising out of her remembering. Towards heat, as heat undulates like a cobra and snakes around her serpentine stem unfurling. Phallic and swelling. The tip blushing. Perfectly tipped, perfectly budded, perfectly pink. Awakening to sun. Awakening to heat. To the scent of her own desire opening.

Thirteen Fairies

There were thirteen fairies at my christening. My dad drank brandy
with a quaalude. My mother baptized me with her tears, wishing she
was closer to her mother. To share my tiny pink unwrinkled, old man
turtle wisdom face with her.

The stars were golden on the sidewalks. You came from the stars,
said the thirteenth fairy. And I landed in the city with golden stars.
Hollywood, California. Someday I'll go back to the stars. Someday
I'll be a star myself, radiating the night with shimmers of possibility.
For now, it's a lot of falling and rising. It's a lot of changing patterns
and waking. I always had a small pointy head and I think too much.
But if you put the human body into the shape of the Vitruvius man,
the body arms wide legs open, head at the very top, the crown —a
five pointed star. I have a pointy star head and my grandma's pointy
chin. I wear her worry and her difficulty seeing far. But I am a seer.
She was too. The more you resist, the stronger glasses prescription
you need. I wear her rigidity in my bones. It's a lot of work to soften
black and white stories. To bring in colors. Hues. Depth. Texture. To
fall to earth, flat and rise up, to fill, to deepen. To round. To shape the
contours with shadows and be okay with that.

What I really want to say is this: my life story is a wackadoodle,
wackamole, guacamole Holy Moly story of small town girl rooted to
broken poor, Catholic old school, redneck hick, who'sville here'sville
yooper-ness. With many many calls to adventure to reclaim my red
velvet cape. To fuck the wolf and grow fur on the right side of my
body. Or perhaps the left. To discover the sword of my pen and
wield it for power. To rewrite my destiny, tame and transform the old
stories. The thirteenth fairy is now my closest sister. Seen. Not seen.
Known. Not know. Mysterious and wise. Faithful, steadfast and true.

Lost Father

Lost lost lost

but how did I get here -flying by the seat of my pants, by the seat of fire. Deep into the thick thicket of woods. But the hind was so glorious bounding off into the ripe unknown. Chasing her white tail. Smelling her fear. Tasting her heat. I was already lost in the chase, lost in the hunt, lost in the ecstasy of being alive. The more ecstatic, the more true, and the more ego-less.

And I found myself
Lost in the woods
With a witch
No way out
But a black witch
For a bride

Seduced by the wrong side of luck. Why should I find myself in these woods alone meeting the Dark Side of the Moon. They say karma comes any which way. She found me.
Patterns. Wheels. Cycles. Scraps.

Spinning round
The twist of time
Twist of fate
Rhyme — No Rhyme.

Patterns. Wheels. Cycles. Scraps.

Vow

I took a vow of silence for more than six years. I vowed not to see, not to hear, not to know the Holy, Holy Irrational Knowings beyond the veil. Beyond Knowing. Inside a culture not supportive of the Wild Holy seer. *Ver. Verla.* Viking Seer - yes. But lineage shrinks from the Holy Holy. I was a seer. I am a seer. I am not afraid to see. I am not afraid of my mind. I am no longer afraid of this Holy Calling.

I hear. I sense I see. Things that I cannot see. I saw things I should not have seen in childhood. Traumatic things I wasn't supposed to know.

I was imprisoned in previous lifetimes. I was crazy went crazy. Feared insanity. Tortured to death. Went insane. Experienced broken, traumatic past lives. I am now safe.

Brother Swan where do you fly?
Brother Swan what do you see?
Brother Swan what do you know?

Truth in Sky. White Holy Clouds
Freedom in Flight
Bondage to Sky
Always flying

What did she see when so so young,
that she wasn't supposed to see?

Wild Eros

I'm having an unexpected awakening of Eros.
Divine timing full moon magical rhythm
 is sparking at Eros threads. It's written in the stars.
For some Eros is lust and sex, love and attraction.
And it does express this aspect well.
To draw opposites together.
Or generate new sparks for new life,
new creations (babies or creative babies)
to illuminate hidden things, shadows, restrictions, exaggerations.
And more. Eros.
And psyche. What happens to the psyche when Eros stirs?
What happens to Eros when psyche doubts.
Oh the journey in this myth is a painful journey.
A beautiful journey. A terrifying journey.
A journey with unexpected twists and turns.

I used to dive deeply into the scent of this story-
years and years and years ago.
Hungry then to understand psyche, to understand Eros.
Perhaps this hunger led me towards depth psychology
understanding in fairytale and myth.
Thank you Eros
for compelling me always
ever exploring more in the universe of your expression.

But also Eros sleeps in me.
Goes numb. Cold. Foreign. A gated landscape.
And sometimes, in the timing of things, the briar patch simply opens
and beauty awakens. Thank you Eros in fairytale- water of life.
Catalyst of alchemical awakenings.

Eros. Hunger to know *dusha* (soul in a foreign language)

Eros. Hunger to understand the deeper and higher impulse beneath
attraction and Eros. Above Eros and attraction.
Always more than meets the eye.
Intent on making us come alive.

It's been sparked. Eros is always sparking.
Better to say- I'm paying attention.
Nature can spark us. The moon can spark us.
A rainstorm can spark. A new friend can spark.
An illuminating conversation. There are many sparks.
Eros is sparky. It doesn't always lead us on a straight line
to what it wants to uncover and transform in self.
It's a mystery.
But I like the spark of life. Of Eros.

I like how it urges towards the mysterious scent of all things
towards the jaguar breath of coming to life,
towards the primal and the spiritual the sensual and the awakened.

Revisiting the myth. Just because.
Because...The world might need saving.
From its mechanical erosion of eros.
Spark! Flowers bloom. Spark! Butterflies emerge. Spark!
A conversation breathes new possibilities into creation. Spark!
Alchemy. Spark! Unexpected awakening.

What is your relationship to Eros? To Eros and psyche
To myth and meaning when it comes to awakening and enlivening?

Dare I say...here's to penetrating
the depths and heights
Of love. Of Eros.
Of ancient fairytales sparking new awakening.

I've been touched by a Cupid's spell.

Advice from a Swan

how to transcend a story:

1. lift the story up out of itself and look at it objectively
2. be compassionate
3. love yourself and the story
4. let it go
5. trust the wings of the story. it will soar

love is the wind
and breath
that purifies and moves all things

Five Minutes of Life

The contractions were long and short and quickened. This star was ready or not here I come. There was no, 'trust me child'. There were no 13 fairies or fronds in the lily pond. There was muck and a chain round my neck, choking the cry, choking the words. But it was full throttle. 1, 2, 3 go. I was induced because Dr. Zimmerman wanted to have a vacation. It was close to new year's eve. He didn't want to birth me while partying with the other doctors and wives. So I came early. Sped up. Falling star. Flat lined. Run for cover. He caught her. She looked wrinkled tiny puckered plucked mid air. It hurts my arm to catch a story like this. It goes so fast and yet still there is so much time to Catch my breath. To catch kisses. To catch trouble. To catch mystery. To catch disease. To catch karma. To catch mice. To catch tigers by the tail. Poetry —all goddamned all of it. How can I forget that each story flung to me is flung by a god I ignore. Each story clean as a whistle after I let it blow its merry piper's tune dirge.

Story. Boats. Journeying across the sea.

Daughters, the Women are Speaking

What are they speaking of?

We've traveled off the path and into the belly of the wolf. Where it was dark and scary in the dark with grandmother stories. We meandered into the woods with the pukwudginee. Beyond the birdsong wilderness where all went to sleep for 100 years, surrounded by hedges, briars, thorns, roses. We journey into blooms.

We were lost again. Journeyed into curses. Hexes. Evil stepmothers. We lost our brothers. We were the lost brothers, became swans, we dreamed into otherworld. We vowed silence. We worked with our hands. We were married and bore children while grieving, while working tirelessly to break spells, to heal family. We were the 13th fairy, uninvited. We inherited difficult family stories. We worked hard to rise up despite struggle. We lost mothers, fathers, kingdoms, clothing. We gave blood. We longed for new babies. Our stories were slandered misrepresented. We were innocent. We stumbled and gained wisdom. We lost our way. We followed the voice of the doll in our pockets to the hut of mystery of supernatural remembering. We sorted. We cleaned seeds. We served the great dark goddess. We killed the wolf. We skinned him alive after killing his belly with stones. We wove sigils with our hands. We were given an almighty burning skull. We carried it with humility and reverence. We grew courage.

We told stories.

Water Story

I am the purity of the well. I am the water cleansing the tears that have dried up. I am the well of longing for belonging and home. In every woman. In every body. I am the longing and the source of renewal. Of remembering. I am the voice of grief. I am the voice of hope.

I have travelled deeply, deeply beneath the roots. To the world tree. There, a dragon has gnawed at me. There the fates still weave. There are beautiful patterns in the weaving and there are challenging knots. Knotted before time as we know it.

This dragon ravishes the roots. The leaves are withering, curling, browning, falling. The Norns replenish the roots but the leaves are not yet budding. It is a difficult time to be a woman. There are many difficult stories. There is wasteland and there are lies in so many parts of the world. In almost every corner. It encroaches. I am a well maiden. I am a woman of the well. I have been hiding. My daughter is a well maiden. She hides too. I hide her from view.

Is it safe to emerge? Can I share the cup of this source? How do I remain open? How do I continue to wear white? My dress has turned black. This is a difficult turning point. I am not alone. Woman —do you hear me? What do you know? How do you see the way forward? What is your grief story?

Why is there so much evil and destruction? Why must so much innocence be taken? Why must the land be broken? Why must the stories be so difficult? I ached when I read Sharon Blackie's well maiden story. I ached for the gift of the well maidens. I ached for their disappearance. I ache for their loss. I ache for their hiding. I ache for their rape. Persephone. Rape was literally seeded into you. Is this the way of the patriarchy? Is this the way? To be led by the Broken King?

I ache for the hunger for the restoration of the world. I ache with longing to be restored. I ache with longing for the children of the world to taste the well of truth.

This is my deep grief. To live in a world where the well has run dry. Is poisoned. Is forgotten. What if I am now the source of this well? What must I do to keep it flowing? To keep it pure? To keep it honest? To keep it alive and well?

How do I serve this sacred well? How do I serve others from the well?

Hide and Seek

My day is spent searching for wisdom. A baby deer curled up in the tall, tall apple green grass. A poem, quietly secreted away. My day is spent searching for answers to the questions without words. Searching for sight. Searching for knowing. Searching for truth. Searching for stories. Catching threads of meaning. Catching a whiff of the shape of scents like cinnamon. Watermelon. Lily. My day is spent harnessing, wielding the tension in the grasses. Wilding the opposites. Weaving willow branches in my mind, wishing I too could weave twig and bark and mend the world. Carry her in a basket make the disparate parts whole. Make her beauty visible. Make her story softer, more pliable. Rounder. A gift. To carry other stories.

All of It: Revisiting Beauty

Beauty is human. So is suffering. Listening is an act of love. Presence is powerful. These bodies contain infinite possibilities as well as multitudes of broken stories. We repair the world when we weave the threads of our stories together again. There is medicine in remembering: within every human being is a story of isolation, grief, sadness and pain. Within every human is a story of loss, forgetting and sleep.

Thorns, tangles, and hedges; the pinpricks and the pain. The thirteenth fairy and her curse (perhaps it is the greatest blessing). It's a curse when we forget to invite suffering and pain to the party. Who wants to celebrate those things? But what if the suffering, the pain, the acceptance of these things is really the exquisite eros of experiencing ALLness.

It's a complicated dance. Inside the webs of stories, there are a lot of sticky uncomfortable threads. Sometimes we need to tightrope walk carefully on tip toes across the sticky stories. We can get tangled and dangle in old stories.

Sometimes we need to choose to walk the path of pins or the path of needles. Sometimes we need to walk Beauty for miles, focusing on sensation. Skin, bare feet, soil, soul, breath, body.

Sometimes we need to lean close, tenderly, to the stickiest thread, and listen carefully and compassionately without getting caught in the lies it once spun. Sometimes we need to hold the tension of paradox and opposite together - burden, beast, beauty.

I was made for ALL OF IT.
I was made for ALL OF IT.
I was made for ALL OF IT.

Belly to ground knowing. Sensing red in everything. Animal becoming-human body. Complex mish-mash marriage of ALL OF IT. Because of this, I too, am a divine union. A living, poem. Happily Ever After in flesh, becoming Holy with the Wholeness of my Stories.

The Wheel + Love Notes

We began our writing journey near the Taurus new Moon in May. We completed our process on Llamas, with an online celebration, in which each woman had ten minutes to perform or read selected writings. This book, the elixir of the return journey and the blossom of the creative expression. Born at Winter Solstice (or summer, for our Australian participant).

12 weeks +1, with you —13 of the most amazing women. Special mention to Sequoiah Hummingbird, a participant whose writings are not included in this publication, but who wrote with us from her nest on Madeline Island. Her words rippled waterfalls, grew moss, dappled golden upon oak leaves, fluttered ruby throated and winged and echoed the never-ending blessings of the great Gichi-gami.

All of you. Embroidering poems into my heart. Writing. Righting. Rite-ing your way in and out of Stories. In and through mystery. Arrows. Quivering. Eros. Alive. Sparked.

Retrieving.

Into the forest and out of the belly of the wolf. Liminal edge walkers. Moistened by fairytales.

Into sleep, spindle pricked. Awakened blooms. You hunted and were hunted. You wove swan shirts out of asters, voiceless. You flew with swans. You found voice. Stepmothers and the 13th fairy. Daughters and mothers. A thousand different women. Kings and queens. Lost girls. Swimming with Selkies. Adorned with stinky fox pelts. Becoming Fox woman. Birdsong. Churned and stirred. Shape shifting and shape shifted. Through wastelands and back home to ancient wells. You rose out of the mud, reeking of resurrection. You found yourself inside of revelations.

I am transformed by your beauty. You are Beauty.
Blooms. Holy blossoms. Deepening me.

I was found.
The hot lipped Eros
struck me with a flame tipped pen.
I too bloomed. The red came back into me.

Re-wilded
Re-wed
Re-red

With new life. New words. New colors. New shapes.

Thank you women of Crack Open the Story. Each and every one of
you. I love you. It was the deepest honor to see you. The intimacy of
your opening. To witness the cracking. And behold what emerged.

Your courage. Your vulnerability. Your Eros. Your wild.

I howl new constellations with you. This book, a tapestry of hope.
Singing. Storying the new dawn. Because of you, light is born
brighter out of the dark, dark belly of night.

Thank you.
In gratitude.

Love,
Stasha
and the wild matryoshka
at the center of story

Winter Solstice 2024 (Summer in the Southern Hemisphere)

snip snap snout
this tale is told out

Made in the USA
Las Vegas, NV
21 December 2024

15058645R00134